Income Distribution within Irish Households

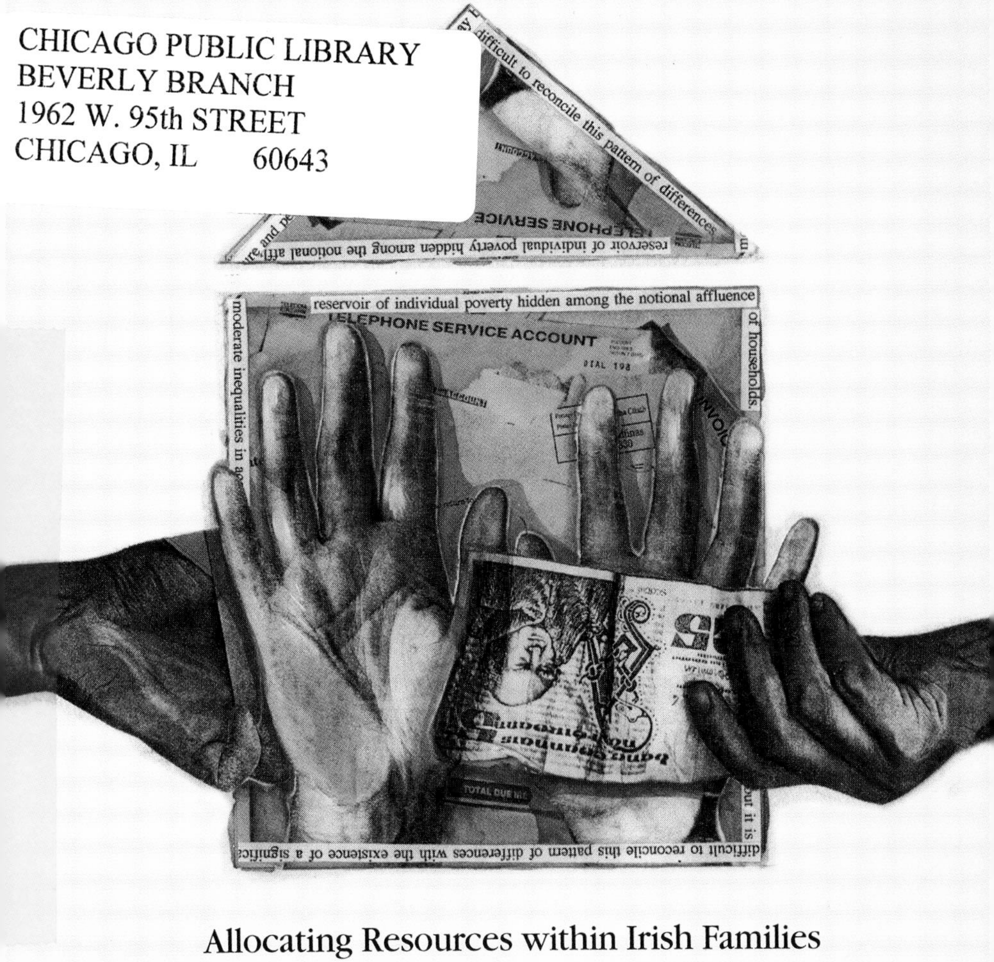

Allocating Resources within Irish Families

David Rottman

Design and Production
Language *visual communications*

Copy Editing
Vaari Claffey

CONTENTS

iii

List of Tables

List of Figures

ACKNOWLEDGMENTS

This report is based on the responses to a survey that was designed by Brendan Whelan, Head of the ESRI Survey Unit. James Williams, also of the ESRI Survey Unit, collated the resulting data into a file suitable for analysis, a formidable challenge. I am grateful to Brendan and James for creating the base of data on which I was able to build, and for their comments on drafts of this report.

Comments and suggestions by Brian Nolan, Pat O'Connor and Jan Pahl are also gratefully acknowledged, along with the statistical advice provided by Gary Keogh. Trutz Haase of the Combat Poverty Agency guided the report through a series of drafts and reviews and Helen Johnston, also of the Agency, brought the report to publication. I stress, however, that all descriptions, assertions, interpretations, and conclusions in the report are entirely my responsibility.

FOREWORD

Social welfare payments are made on the assumption that money will be shared within the household. There is little evidence, however, to support that assumption. David Rottman's pathbreaking study on income distribution and management systems within Irish households allows us to peek into the "black box" of the Irish family to see how resources are managed within households and to examine the standards of living enjoyed by individual members of a household.

The Combat Poverty Agency commissioned this research report from the ESRI to look at income distribution within Irish households. There is a view that a measure of household poverty paints the full picture of the economic and financial circumstances of all members of the household. To some extent an aggregate household measure may mask intra-household poverty; for example, some evidence from the UK suggests that there are substantial gender inequalities in terms of within-household distribution of resources and consumption patterns. This report draws on British literature and ERSI survey data to look at family management systems in Ireland.

This study focuses on the distribution of income within households in general, rather than being concerned specifically with intra-household poverty. This is related to the range of information which was available from the ESRI Household Survey on which this study is based. Nevertheless, this report provides the most detailed insight to date into the family financial arrangements which prevail in Irish households. The study looks at the ways in which income is shared and how responsibilities for different expenditures are divided. The report demonstrates that the variations in the financial management system adopted and actual household outcomes are dependent on a large number of factors including the level of disposable income as well as social class, wife's employment, income source and family cycle.

One of the most important findings in the report is the overwhelming importance of separate incomes to wives, both for their own well-being and for that of their children and, in particular, the importance of Child Benefit. Child Benefit emerges as the sole independent income available to most married women. There is also evidence that women's earnings or income directly received give women greater control over how that money is used. This would support the argument for wives' direct entitlement to benefits.

Access to personal spending money and leisure was found to be a useful indicator of how financial decisions affected the well-being of individual family members. Access to personal spending and leisure tends to favour husbands unless family finances are managed independently. The presence of school age children leads to an apparent shift in women's personal spending to spending on their children. Wives' earnings also tend to supplement general household finances.

On examining the psychological well-being of household members, the study found that what matters is the amount of income that is shared. Substantial sums may be earned by household members, but where money is not made available for common use, women's levels of psychological distress and fatalism are likely to be higher.

While the focus of the study is not specifically on intra-household poverty, the evidence presented in the report does not indicate that substantial numbers of women and children live in hidden poverty. However, the evidence on which this conclusion is based is indirect ie the apparent consensus between spouses on spending priorities, the extent of income sharing, and the inequalities in access to personal spending and leisure. Thus the report concludes that it is unlikely that women and children living in households above the poverty lines live in conditions comparable to those experienced by women and children in households below these lines.

While within the context of the study there is no explicit evidence of hidden poverty within households, households on the lowest income levels and those relying on social welfare payments display a different pattern of income sharing and financial management to other households. Households with income derived mainly from social welfare typically share 33 per cent of their income compared to the average of 63 per cent in other households. Low income may also impose an allocation system on families: essential bills are paid first, leaving no excess money about which decisions need to be, or can be, taken. Thus, management systems in low income households tend to give wives the stressful responsibility of managing expenses for food, fuel and housing.

The general message from this report is that while there is evidence of gender inequalities in the management of, and access to, household finances with men in a much stronger position than women, differences in the standards of living experienced by husbands on the one hand and wives and children on the other are insufficient to confirm claims that studies based on individuals rather than on households will uncover widespread hidden poverty within households. This is not to say that future household surveys should not continue to explore financial management and control within households, with a particular focus on those households managing on low income or social welfare payments.

Combat Poverty Agency
October 1994

INCOME DISTRIBUTION WITHIN IRISH HOUSEHOLDS

Executive Summary

Rationale and Background

This is a study of how Irish families organise their finances, based on the responses given by a random sample of 625 couples to a survey in 1989. The key concerns are the degree to which spouses share their incomes, how husbands and wives divide responsibility for household expenditure and the manner in which spending decisions are made.

The first rationale for the study is that social policies, and particularly state transfer programmes, make assumptions about what will happen to money that is given to individual household members. The basic and benevolent assumption is that the money will be shared.

The second basic rationale for the study is that social policy also makes assumptions about who takes responsibility for coping with household spending needs. The role of income provider is one aspect of that responsibility but managing a household budget is arguably more important in terms of the quality of life experienced by individual family members.

Four basic systems for household financial management have been identified in other countries: (1) whole wage systems, in which one spouse, usually the wife, is given full responsibility for expenditure (where the husband is the manager the wife may have no access to cash); (2) allowance systems, in which the main earner makes a set amount available for housekeeping and retains the remainder for (usually) designated expenditure areas; (3) joint management, with pooled finances to which both spouses, in principle, have equal access, and (4) independent management, applicable to those two earner households in which neither partner has access to all of the household finances.

The main determinants of the financial management system a household adopts are thought to be (a) income level; (b) income source; and (c) social class. In particular, a low household income is associated with whole wage/wife control financial management systems in which the husband is responsible only for personal spending; high incomes encourage husband control through an allowance system in which he is responsible for major expenditure items, such as rent.

Sharing is more common where the wife has an income, with wife controlled pooling at medium income levels and husband controlled pooling at higher income levels being the norm. However, where wives make a substantial contribution to household income, independent management prevails. There is evidence that where the wife makes the largest contribution to household income, household finances are managed jointly but without additional control accruing to the wife. Husband's earnings appear more likely than wives' earnings to confer ownership rights that translate into control.

Financial management systems have been shown to affect the financial and psychological well-being of wives and husbands. Wife management and wife control are associated with husbands spending more on leisure than wives; this also occurs in households using an allowance system. Joint management generates a more equitable distribution of spending on leisure. Management systems in low income households tend to give wives the stressful responsibility of managing the expenses for food, fuel and housing.

Given the experience of research conducted elsewhere, viewed through the lens of specifically Irish socio-economic circumstances and social policy concerns, it seems sensible to focus on two main aspects of family finances. First, how much of income is being shared in Irish households? Sharing means that money is set aside for the "common good", rather than retained by individual earners. Secondly, how is responsibility for making expenditure decisions divided in Irish households?

Income Sharing and Expenditure Responsibilities in Irish Families

In 1989, half of Irish couples surveyed used a whole wage management system with wife control, (equivalent to one person management); a further 5 per cent represented an allowance system with husband control, (equivalent to main earner control); nearly 40 per cent of households used joint management in the form of an allowance system with a "kitty" or allowance that was supplemented by direct purchase of some essential items by the main earner; and in one household in ten independent management prevailed.

The prevalence of various types of financial management systems in Ireland appears to be quite different from what is reported in British studies. In the mid-1980s whole wage systems were scarce in Britain, being present in about one out of every six households. Allowance based systems were more common, but represented only one out of every four households. Half of British households used a joint management system, and one out of twelve practiced independent management.

Some form of income sharing can be found in the overwhelming majority of Irish families. One or more household members paid an allowance or contribute to a household kitty in 85 per cent of families. Members of Irish families, on average, shared an estimated 55 per cent of their incomes. Most of that shared income is used to pay for basic costs of living. In the average family, the cost of the week's groceries (defined as "food and household essentials") was equivalent to 59 per cent of the amount being shared.

Husbands and wives generally agreed in their assessments of family finances and their spending priorities. Differences follow patterns found by research elsewhere: wives are more child-orientated when describing their spending priorities.

Sharing of resources within the family is less equitable. Husbands are consistently more likely to have access to money for their own entertainment and to have more money to spend on leisure whenever like households are compared with like. Thus, even where both husband and wife work and both have access to personal spending money, the husbands have the larger share. Generally though, the differences between husbands and wives are not substantial.

Influences on the Income Sharing and Financial Management System
The top and the bottom of the income distribution are distinctive in the degree to which independent management is practised in the former and wife management in the latter. Wife managed households are most common at the bottom of the income distribution being found in 59 per cent of bottom quintile households and 36 per cent of top quintile households. Husband management is twice as common in the bottom as in the top quintile. Independent management is found in only 7 per cent of the bottom quintile households and 18 per cent of the top.

The division of expenditure responsibilities follows traditional gender-based distinctions in which wives, as household managers, take primary responsibility for day to day essentials and husbands for large recurrent expenses, such as rent.

Income sharing is low in high income households (where 40 per cent of household income is made available for common use) and in low income households (where on average 50 per cent is shared). Sharing is thus most prevalent at the middle of the income distribution, where, on average, household members share 70 per cent of their combined incomes.

Households with income derived mainly from social welfare payments typically share 33 per cent of their income, compared to the average of 63 per cent in other households. The extent of sharing is slightly higher in households where women are in paid employment and in farm households.

Consequences of Financial Management Systems

Overall sharing of expenditure responsibilities appears to be more consequential for what occurs within families than the degree of income sharing itself. The level of disagreement on financial matters, spending priorities, and the equity with which personal leisure and personal spending money are distributed are all strongly associated with how expenditure responsibilities are divided.

The type of financial management system adopted has a particularly strong influence on the amount of personal spending money available to women, and serves as a better predictor of that amount than total household income. Much of the effect is due to low levels of personal spending money in husband controlled households and high levels of personal spending money in independently managed households. Average amounts of personal spending money per week are: whole wage system £10.67; allowance-based system £6.20; joint management £12.35; and independent management £22.06, (1989).

For the psychological well-being of household members, what matters is that amount of income that is shared. Substantial sums may be earned by household members but where it is not made available for common use women's levels of psychological distress and feelings of fatalism are likely to be higher than otherwise would be the case.

Women's Incomes and Child Benefit

Among households receiving Child Benefit, 58 per cent of women have no other source of income; in 10 per cent there is income from employment or interest, which on a weekly basis is less than what Child Benefit provides; and women's earnings in 32 per cent of households exceed the amount of Child Benefit.

Women's incomes are largely devoted to family rather than personal expenditures, and there is an equally strong tendency for that contribution to go to general purposes. The presence of school age children leads to an apparent shift from personal spending to spending on the children. Wives' earnings, therefore, supplement general household finances.

The control and use of Child Benefit payments is of particular interest because it is the one source of state income support that is paid directly to the mother. In most households the wife controls the use of Child Benefit. Where women make the financial decisions regarding Child Benefit, 46 per cent of households claim that the money goes for general housekeeping and 44 per cent for child specific expenses. The corresponding breakdown for jointly managed households is 75 per cent and 18 per cent.

Wives also tend to share more of their earnings than their husbands do. The proportion of the wives' income that is shared is affected by dependent children. This is evident in the relationship between the amount of the woman's income and the percentage of that income spent on personal items. Higher earnings lead to larger percentages being spent on personal clothing and leisure only if there are no children resident.

In households where women decide how to spend Child Benefit payments, 22 per cent of husbands and 30 per cent of wives chose a child-specific item as their first priority for an increase to the households regular income. That was the first priority for 15 per cent of husbands and 23 percent of wives in households where the decision on how to spend Child Benefit was made jointly.

The survey results do not lend credence to claims that substantial numbers of Irish women and children live in "hidden poverty", hidden because conventional studies of poverty attribute a household's income to all of its members. This emerges from indirect evidence on consensus between spouses on financial matters, the extent of income sharing, and the moderate inequalities in access to leisure and personal spending money. Indirect it may be, but it is difficult to reconcile this pattern of differences with the existence of a significant reservoir of individual poverty hidden among the notional affluence of households.

Still, some types of households were identified where high incomes may indeed mask intra-household poverty: where Child Benefit is spent jointly or where the husband is both the main earner and the household manager. Such households, however, are relatively rare.

CHAPTER ONE

Introduction and Summary

1. Rationale for the Study

This is a study of how Irish families organise their finances, based on the responses given by a random sample of couples to a survey in 1989. The key concerns are the degree to which spouses share their incomes, how husbands and wives divide responsibility for making household expenditures and the manner in which spending decisions are made. In using the survey results to pursue those three key concerns, the intention is both to describe those aspects of family finances, and to offer an explanation for why families differ in those respects. Whether such differences affect the well-being of family members will also be examined.

Specific questions addressed by the study include:
Who takes overall responsibility for managing the household finances?
How much of the household's income is made available for common needs?
Does responsibility for managing the finances bring with it control over the uses of family money?
Do earners within a family contribute equally to general household expenses and to the costs of child rearing?
Who retains money over which they have discretion?
Where income is limited relative to a family's needs, who makes the sacrifices that allow ends to be met and who carries the psychological burden of coping?

The answers to such questions are of direct relevance to current debate about social policy in this country. There are two basic ways in which family financial management is relevant to how public policy in the 1990s affects the well-being of family members. These provide the primary rationale for conducting research on family financial management, although a less practical rationale based on the contribution to what we know about family dynamics is also advanced.

The first rationale is that social policies, and particularly state transfer programmes, make assumptions about what will happen to money that is given to individual household members. The basic and benevolent assumption is that the money will be shared (Piachuad, 1987). To the degree that money is not shared, policy objectives are not being met and, indeed, other family problems are being reinforced or created. Consequently, family finances are an integral component of any programme for studying poverty and low incomes. This study offers estimates on the extent of income sharing in Irish households.

Estimates of sharing will have potential implications for the study of poverty in this country. Conventional or "mainstream" approaches to measuring poverty define a poverty line and then assume that all individuals living in households with incomes above that line are out of poverty (Jenkins, 1991). However, it can be argued that individuals (in practice, women and children) living in households with moderate to high levels of disposable incomes may experience deprivation if income is not being shared or being spent in an equitable manner. Conversely, individuals (men) living in low income households may escape poverty through unequal sharing. This study offers a first look at whether important intra-household inequalities were ignored in previous studies of Irish poverty levels and composition. To obtain the desired estimates however, requires that we look at the situations of households over the full income spectrum, rather than those falling below a particular "poverty line".

The Irish social insurance and social welfare system, like that in most western European countries, divides payments between a fixed sum for the individual recipient and smaller amounts for each adult or child dependent on the recipient. In the tradition of the Beveridge Report, which had a major impact on Ireland, there remains the vestige of the belief that a husband's secure employment is a married woman's "first line of defence" against poverty and other contingencies (quoted in Kennedy, 1989:88). That recipients may share varying proportions of their individual entitlement is not, for the most part, regarded as the State's business, nor is the actual use made of monies provided for dependent spouses or children.

Child Benefit in Ireland is a partial exception in that it is paid directly to the mother (as provided by the Social Welfare Act, 1974). Subsequent proposals to unify State child support payments and place them in the control of mothers working in the home have not been implemented (eg Building on Reality, 1984; NESC, 1990:224-5). The Review Group on the Treatment of Households in the Social Welfare Code was asked (in 1989) to look at issues relating to the entitlement of both spouses in a marriage to be primary recipients. That Review did not recommend establishing an individual entitlement for those currently regarded as adult dependants. However, the prospect of a fundamental, if less radical, change was left open:

> While the payment of adult dependent allowances can be said to reflect the family based nature of the existing payment structure, it can also be argued that they also serve to reinforce the notion of dependency of

3

married women engaged in home duties. The Group considers that this negative aspect of the existing structure could be minimised, however, by entitling the adult dependant to a share of the overall payment in his or her own right (1991:5.30).

The issue of whether a married couple should be treated as a unit or as individuals is therefore clearly at the top of the social policy agenda for the 1990's. EC directives, such as that on Equal Social Security Rights, articulate a rationale that does not discriminate between market incomes and caring. Indeed, the ideas of social citizenship that underlie most contemporary social insurance and social welfare programmes strongly support such an equality between work and caring, but the principle is rarely implemented in practice (Lister, 1990).

The second basic rationale for the study is that social policy also makes assumptions about who takes responsibility for coping with household spending needs. The role of income provider is one aspect of that responsibility. But managing a household budget is arguably more important in terms of the quality of life experienced by individual family members. Responsibility for financial management is also likely to be stressful, especially in households with low incomes or in which income is inadequate relative to family needs. There is a tendency to assume that such stress, like income, is shared. Consequently, research can inform social policy by making transparent the lines of responsibility for financial management. This allows us to see how purchasing power is in fact distributed among family members and also where the stresses and strains of coping on low incomes are concentrated.

There is yet another, more abstract, rationale for conducting a study of family finances in Ireland. Money can reveal important aspects of family life that are otherwise obscure. Arguably, we cannot hope to fully understand how families function unless we can trace the way in which money is earned and then spent. Tracing the flows of money into and out of a household and determining who decides how it will be spent can indicate the degree of equality and the division of power between spouses.

Domestic money is a special money, not just a medium of economic exchange but a meaningful, socially constructed currency, shaped by the domestic sphere where it circulates and by the gender and social class of its domestic money handlers (Zelizer, 1989:369-70).

In this study the use of domestic money offers a window into decision-making within families, with particular emphasis on who makes that type of decision.

So this third, less practical rationale is that a study of financial management rounds out our understanding of families as income generating and spending units. Consequently, while the theme of the report is financial management, a running subplot is the sharing of important decisions by husbands and wives. The results of any one research effort will be too tentative and too partial for use as a guide to specific policies. Rather, the research can raise some questions abut how closely family behaviour conforms to the images that we use in thinking about the family and how social policy affects the family. Thus, here too, research on family financial arrangements ultimately connects back to public policy. Research carried out internationally, for example, consistently suggests that

> the distribution of power in the family changes in favour of the wife wherever she contributes financially to the household (Coser, 1990:71).

Another apparent truism is that, given the existence of discretionary family expenditure, the responsibility for consumption tends to confer power on wives. Where such discretionary income is lacking, consumption responsibility becomes an additional burden for wives. Generally therefore, wive's control over consumption tends to translate into power and greater equality in middle class families but acts to the detriment of the position of wives in low income households.

What all three rationales have in common is that internal workings of what is a "black box" in most studies of poverty and income adequacy will be, at least partly, revealed. This permits us to link the amounts and sources of income entering the household more precisely to the standard of living enjoyed by individual members of a household.

1.1 Outline of the Report

The above concerns and questions are examined in the following manner. This chapter provides an introduction by reviewing previous research and considering its applicability to Ireland. Some important terms are defined and some expectations derived about what the study will find. Chapter 2 then describes the data that are available for the study, noting the possibilities and limitations for a study of family financial management.

Chapter 3 begins the formal consideration of what the data have to say on the extent of income sharing and the division of expenditure responsibilities in Ireland. Chapter 4 offers a profile of financial decision-making in Irish households. This includes a description of the degree to which spouses agree on spending priorities and in their assessments of the household financial situation, and, more generally, the extent of consensus among husbands and wives on financial matters.

Chapter 5 switches the focus to differences among families: the types of families that have particular degrees of income sharing and particular forms of family financial management and financial decision-making. For example, households at particular income levels and relying on similar income sources may evidence common patterns of financial management. Similarly, methods of family financial management may be typical of specific social classes or stages of the family cycle. Particular attention is placed on multi-earner households to trace the impact that access to income has on the distribution of decision-making power and the distribution of money within the household.

Chapter 6 looks at the consequences of different degrees of income sharing and methods of financial management for the economic and psychological well-being of family members. Material consequences include the objective level of deprivation experienced by a household, the proportion of income allocated for essential housekeeping expenses, and the distribution between the spouses of personal spending money and leisure time activities. Socio-emotional consequences include the level of psychological distress experienced by spouses and their sense of fatalism or control over their circumstances. Here, cause and effect may link three sets of household factors: (1) family socio-economic circumstances, (2) financial management systems, and (3) the standard of living that family members individually and collectively enjoy. It is possible that the implications of income size and stability for household well-being may be mediated by the way in which families make financial decisions.

Chapter 7 then narrows the focus to a specific but crucial problem: the impact of wive's earnings and Child Benefit on family finances, and the implications that dependent children have for family financial management. A final chapter relates the information and analyses in Chapters 2 - 7 back to the concerns raised in this introductory chapter. The report is prefaced by a summary of the main findings and conclusions.

1.2 Ideas and Assumptions

Given the objectives of the study, families will be portrayed primarily as economic units:

> private associations of people who share resources and tasks (even if they don't share them fairly) (Smith, 1992:92).

Such a narrow economic portrayal is appropriate because it is through family units that income, derived from employment (or self-employment) and from social welfare entitlements, is distributed more widely to people who are not in employment or who are without entitlements in their own right. Adopting this view of the Irish family does not require that we become burdened with implicit assumptions about who works or should work, what constitutes paid work, who has entitlements, or who takes responsibilities for home duties such as child-rearing. But we do need to acknowledge that the study is set in a society within which work, income and responsibilities are divided among family members in particular ways that can be regarded as typical; men tend to work and have entitlements; women tend to depend on redistribution of their husband's income within the family.

An extensive and deeply entrenched foundation supports and maintains that typical family economic structure. Again, the objectives of the study direct our attention narrowly toward those ways in which state policies tend to reinforce certain patterns. Two aspects are of special interest. One is the consistent and fundamental distinction in state policy between being in the workforce and being engaged in home duties, with those in home duties dependent on agreement that sufficient income will be shared.[1] This applies whether income is from employment or from social welfare, because payments for dependants are made to the person with entitlements. The exception is Child Benefit, which is paid directly to the mother, and is typically the sole source of independent income accruing to married women not in the labour force. The second distinction is embedded in income tax and social welfare policies, which combine to inhibit married women's labour force participation. For example, if the wife of someone who is in receipt of social assistance earns in excess of £55 per week (£60 per week from 1993[2]), her spouse loses the adult dependent's payment. This translates

---

[1]   Marriage entails a legal responsibility on the partners to provide financial support for one another: s 214 (c) and (d) Social Welfare (Consolidation) Act 1981, cited by Fitzgerald (1992:27).

[2]   This income threshold remained unchanged at £60 in the 1994-95 budget.

into the need to secure a job that pays a wage at a rate near the average industrial earnings - roughly £200 weekly[3] - for the family to be as well off financially with her at work as with her in the home (Fitzgerald, 1992).

The view of the family as primarily an economic unit that is shaped by the dictates of state policy may seem excessively narrow and stark. Families are, of course, also units that provide social and emotional support to their members, albeit to varying degrees. Indeed, that aspect of the family is relevant here because of the potential link between, on the one hand, the fairness and efficiency with which the family unit serves to distribute earnings and entitlements and, on the other hand, the quality of emotional and social support that is generated.

Sharing and decision-making, then, are the two aspects of family finances that will be examined most closely. This should not prove excessively restrictive. After all, the extent of income sharing and the division of expenditure responsibilities speak directly to the concerns that have been raised about poverty within families: how much of the family's resources is made available for use by each spouse. Further, sharing of income and of expenditure responsibilities are the most plausible links that have been suggested, tying intra-household income inequalities to the quality of life circumstances experienced by individual family members.

The remainder of this introductory chapter provides an overview of what social science theory and research can provide as markers for this report.

1.3 Theories and Evidence on Household Management
There is a substantial body of thinking and research that may be relevant to a study of financial management in Irish households. The applicability of that material to the concerns of this report, however, needs to be carefully assessed.

There is an established tradition of research on family budgeting dating back to the nineteenth century (LePlay, 1879; Rowntree, 1899) which is gaining prominence with the study of urban industrial workers in the twentieth century (Young and Willmott, 1957: Young, 1952; 1977). Dysfunctional financial management featured, usually in a minor supporting role, in the

---

[3]   Average industrial earnings were approximately £240 per week in 1992, (CSO, 1993:231)

"cycle of poverty" and "culture of poverty" explanations for the persistence of poverty in particular families.

Most recent studies of how families manage their finances are part of a general concern about the effect of economic and social change on family life. Well-established research traditions exist on the impact of economic development in Third World countries and on the advent of two earner marriages in the wealthier countries of the First World. Much of that interest is due to the women's movement, which introduced greater sensitivity to the contribution made by women as earners and as carers. The movement also brought a sceptical view of the degree to which such changes as can be identified actually diverge from traditional divisions of power and responsibility within families in either the First or the Third Worlds.

This section tries to distil what social scientists have found about family financial management in other countries into a framework for conducting research in this country. This is done by answering three basic questions: (1) What methods of financial management do families use? (2) What kinds of families use what types of financial management methods? (3) What are the consequences of adopting a particular type of financial management for family relationships and well-being?

1.3.1. Systems of Financial Management

There is a broad agreement on the existence of four basic systems for household financial management (Pahl, 1989, 1990; Morris, 1990). Management can be through (1) whole wage systems, in which one spouse, usually the wife, is given full responsibility for expenditure (where the husband is the manager, the wife may have no access to cash); (2) allowance systems, in which the main earner makes a set amount available for housekeeping and retains the remainder for (usually) his own designated expenditure spheres; (3) joint management, with pooled finances to which spouses, in principle, have equal access; and (4) independent management, applicable to those two earner households in which neither partner has access to all of the household finances, hence sometimes labelled the "Yuppie system" (Pahl, 1983:245-49). The four systems are claimed to describe the management of finances in, respectively, one sixth, one quarter, one half, and one twelfth of British couples in the mid-1980's, with the whole wage and allowance systems having experienced sharp declines in popularity, and joint management dramatic growth, over recent decades.[4]

Such a classification, it should be made clear, refers to management: to which spouse implements decisions, not to the making of the decisions about how money will be spent. Control is the term used for indicating who makes policy decisions such as spending priorities for the household. Pahl (1989; 1990) proposes that two variables be used when classifying financial management systems to reflect power relationships within families.[5] The first variable is wives' response to the question: Who really controls the money that comes into the household? The result is a dichotomy: households in which the wife claims that she is in control and households in which either the husband is named as being in control or shared control is indicated (either of the latter responses is taken as indicative of husband control on both theoretical and empirical grounds). The second variable is whether there is a joint bank account, taken as indicative of income pooling. Four categories result: wife-control, wife-controlled pooling, husband control and husband controlled pooling.

Is there a sharp distinction between management and control? Pahl's study of 102 couples with dependent children suggests that there is among families that manage on a shared or kitty basis, but not among those on a whole wage or allowance system. The crucial distinction in those households, particularly the latter, is how "spheres of expenditure" for which each spouse takes responsibility are defined. This is a question that Pahl and others working in the area of family finance regard as important but whose implications are as yet only partly incorporated into studies of allocation systems.

There is, as a result, general recognition that existing classifications of allocation systems are imperfect representations of how money gets

---

[4] Morris (1990) usefully cites the UK and USA studies that provide evidence for each finance system. I am grateful to Jan Pahl for drawing my attention to evidence for the dramatic decline in the use by British couples of allowance based systems: Zweig (1961) classified some 69 per cent of couples as using some form of allowance system, a prevalence still little changed in 1968/69 when Townsend's survey was conducted (1979). Current estimates attribute allowance systems to about one quarter of British couples.

[5] Throughout the rest of the report the terms "financial management system" and "allocation system" are used interchangeably.

distributed and spent (see Pahl's frank assessment of her classification scheme, 1989: Chapter 5). Classifications do not manifest consistent relationships to other subjective and objective measures of how money is allocated within households. Moreover, whether questioned jointly or separately, on subjective or factual matters, husbands and wives often give conflicting accounts when describing how they organise their finances. At the same time, answers appear to be conditioned by what is regarded as socially acceptable or correct. It seems sensible to classify as whole wage systems those households in which the husband retains a small personal allowance (Morris, 1990:112). Overall, previous research strongly suggests that while it is difficult to condense the complexities and idiosyncrasies of family finances into a variable with four or five categories, such a representation is a necessary point of departure.

1.3.2 Choice of Financial Management System

The main determinants of which financial management system a household adopts are thought to be (a) social class; (b) income level; (c) wife's employment; (d) income source; and (e) family cycle stage. Here social class stands primarily for gender roles and other culturally defined expectations of family relationships. Class differences capture the variations in household circumstances not attributable to income per se that shape family relationships. The following affinities between household characteristics and financial management systems are drawn from Pahl (1989: Chapters 4 and 6) and Morris (1989: Chapter 2; 1990:110-6), augmented as indicated.

Whereas low household income is associated with whole wage/wife control allocation systems in which the husband is responsible only for personal spending, high incomes encourage husband control through an allowance system in which he is responsible for major expenditure items such as rent and major purchases of consumer durables, particularly if the husband is the sole income earner. Allowance systems allow husbands to retain the returns from additional work effort in, say, overtime hours and to adjust their efforts to meet their personal expenditure needs. Sharing is more common where the wife has an independent income, with wife controlled pooling at medium income levels and husband controlled pooling at higher income levels being the norm. However, independent management prevails where wives make a substantial contribution to household incomes. There is evidence that where the wife makes the largest contribution to household income, household finances are managed jointly without additional control accruing to the wife

(McRae, 1987). Husbands' earnings appear more likely than wives' earnings to confer ownership rights that translate into control. Consequently, where the husband is the main income earner, husband control may occur in households that existing classifications treat as "shared" or "pooled" financial management (Burgoyne, 1990).

The existence of discretionary income for use on major expenditure is the underlying factor. Where such expenditures are possible, male control tends to predominate; where income precludes such purchases, female control results. Generally therefore, the higher a household's income, the more involved husbands become in financial management.

Where income is primarily or entirely in the form of social welfare payments, the predominant form of allocation system is the whole wage system with wife control (Morris, 1984). The source of household income will also be important where one or more members are self-employed, in that business accounts are often interconnected with household finances. Self-employment tends, as a result, to be associated with husband control and management.

Social class is related in a practical manner to the operative management system: cash payment and weekly, rather than monthly, payments tend to promote whole wage and allowance systems. Skilled manual workers are portrayed as likely to use an allowance system; semi-skilled and unskilled workers, whole wage systems. A switch from whole wage to allowance systems has been observed for working class families in which income rises. Middle class ideologies about the family and middle class specific gender roles are more conducive to sharing arrangements.

Financial management systems appear to change over the family cycle (Burgoyne, 1990), although to date the evidence pertains mainly to changes in labour force status associated with child rearing. There are some patterns, however. The presence of dependent children tends to reinforce the tendency for wives to manage and control family finances in low income households. Joint, and particularly independent, management systems are more likely to be found among young couples. Retirement may occasion a shift from joint or independent management to the whole wage system (Morris, 1989:25).

The main consistencies, therefore, relate to the availability of discretionary income and to income adequacy:

spending decisions involving large amounts of money are taken by men, whilst day-to-day budgeting tends to be the responsibility of women....There are a number of ways in which position in the labour market comes to influence a household's financial arrangements. Simply put, these largely relate to size and source of income. The larger the income the more involvement the man has in household financial affairs, arguably because of the greater capacity for spending in large amounts - a characteristically male preserve. The smaller the income the closer total income is to the level required for minimal domestic needs and the more likely it is to be managed by the woman. This is especially true in cases of benefit dependence. Women's earnings at the lower level do little to affect these patterns ...... though at a higher level of status and income women's employment brings a greater probability that there will be some shared element in the overall management of finances (Morris, 1990:193-4).

On this basis, financial management systems are tied closely to a family's income level and income source, and to its social class.

1.3.3 The Implications of Financial Management Systems

The framework for most research on household resource allocation links three clusters of factors. First, households are differently placed in the economy, as manifest in their social class, labour force participation, and income, and differently composed as social units, as manifest in their family cycle stage and composition. Secondly, income is controlled, budgeted, and spent through financial management systems. Thirdly, household members experience varying amounts of material and psychological well-being.

In looking at the consequences of adopting particular allocation systems, one research focus is on how households distribute the "excess" available after paying for essentials. That the "excess" is not equally available to all household members offers one line of research inquiry. Its applicability extends beyond affluent households, because there is potential disagreement within virtually all households as to what counts as the "excess" and what are the priorities for household spending:

> Numerous studies have shown that within many marriages husbands have greater control of resources and have more access to money for social expenditure ... This is particularly likely where husbands are the sole income earners ... But even where they are not, the dominant domestic ideology, with its emphasis on men as income earners and

wives as household servicers encourages the view that men have a greater right to spend time and money on leisure... (Allan, 1989:35-6).

Financial management systems are therefore linked to economic consequences. Where the husband both controls and manages day to day purchases, there is
> likely to be extreme inequality between husband and wife and deprivation on the part of the wife and children (Pahl, 1989:91).

The impact of such inequalities can be dramatic. Among urban Brazilians
> unearned income in the hands of the mother is estimated to have a bigger impact on her family's health than income attributed to the father. For child survival probabilities, the effect is almost 20 times bigger (Thomas, 1990:660).[6]

More generally, the proportion of total household income placed into the housekeeping budget is significantly higher in wife-controlled than in husband-controlled allocation systems (Pahl, 1989:137-9). However, studies thus far have not taken into account the possibility that the correlation may be spurious, attributable to the interrelationship of three factors: household income level, husband control of finances, and the proportion of income allocated to housekeeping.

Spending time on leisure has been shown to vary with allocation system in an interesting manner. Wife management and wife control are associated with husbands spending more than wives on leisure; this also occurs in households using an allowance system. Joint management generates a more equitable distribution of spending on leisure (Pahl, 1989:150).

In poor households, allocation systems operate to make the wife primarily responsible for the crucial, and often substantial, expenses of fuel and housing (Pahl, 1989:145-6). Previous ESRI research has noted the high rates of psychological distress among wives in households where the husband is unemployed and the household is in poverty. The ESRI has explained this in terms of economic exigencies (Whelan and Hannan, Creighton, 1991). Certainly wife control does not itself translate into a more equitable distribution of personal spending money between the spouses: the disparity

---

[6]   Lee and Gibney (1989) provide a study of the nutritional consequences of unemployment and low incomes in a suburb of Dublin.

in favour of the husband tends to be largest in households with wife management and/or control of finances (Volger, 1989:18).

There is some evidence to suggest that the type of allocation system a household uses affects the level of financial deprivation experienced by husbands and wives. One of the few large surveys of allocation systems (1,200 British families) found that the most substantial differences between spouses in financial deprivation occurred in wife-controlled whole wage or pooled systems and in allowance systems (Vogler, 1989:17).

Similarly, in households using whole wage or allowance systems, women's income from employment tends to supplement basic housekeeping. This stems in a fairly straightforward manner from greater income relative to needs or the inadequacy of the household allowance provided.

This accumulation of research findings, drawn primarily but not exclusively from British studies, leads to a paradox. Wife management or wife control of household finances appears to reflect, and perhaps reinforce, gender inequalities in society, not to diminish them. Women have the greatest say in those households in which there is the least to control: low income households, especially those dependent on social welfare, and households raising young children. The absence of wife control might lead to a still less fortunate situation in terms of the circumstances of the wives and children in those households, but responsibility brings burdens rather than enhanced power or equality. Shared or pooled finances may indicate a more equitable distribution of power as well as resources within the household, but the evidence accumulated thus far suggests that such households divide into male-controlled, female-controlled, and jointly-controlled finances. Again, the definition of distinct "spheres of expenditure" responsibility is likely to be crucial for understanding the financial arrangements in these households.

Finally, there is evidence to suggest that Child benefit payments are of particular importance to women in households with wife management or allowance systems. This extends to high income households in which the allocation system is husband controlled:

> Child benefit is particularly valued, not only by women in low income households, but also by women whose husbands exercise a high degree of control over the family budget, even though the household income may be quite large. These women would lose a valued source of income

if Child Benefit were to be means-tested and paid only to poorer families (Pahl, 1989:160-1).

This highlights the importance of looking at what happens to money within the family for understanding the impact of state policy and the relationship between household income and the financial well-being of individual family members.

1.4 Developing a Research Framework for Ireland

No previous research in Ireland describes how families manage their finances.[7] Studies from other countries are typically based on a small number of families with particular characteristics, such as two-earner middle class households or families of a skilled manual group such as coal miners. As a result, those studies can provide little useful guidance as to what one is likely to find in the generality of Irish households. There are, therefore, grounds for scepticism about how applicable the findings of previous research are to Ireland. The usefulness of existing research studies on financial management systems within households is limited because many of these studies have been designed and conducted in societies quite different from Ireland. Furthermore, small scale studies of selected types of households have not, particularly in recent years, been sensitive to variations that might exist in the allocation systems used by households in poverty.

There are a number of practical problems that arise for the study of resource allocation systems in Irish households. First, a large proportion of Irish households remain entirely cash economies: nearly half of all households (47 per cent) did not have a current bank account in 1987 (CSO, 1989:26).[8] This restricts the applicability of Pahl's revised classification, which uses a joint bank account to indicate income sharing. Moreover, the value of Pahl's approach is diminished to the extent that income level, one of the main factors explaining the choice of allocation system, is being incorporated into the allocation measure: households without a bank account by her definition cannot share.

---

[7] The significant exception is research on farm families (eg, Hannan and Katsiaouni, 1977).

[8] A similar percentage of Irish households (47 per cent) do not have a bank deposit account (Nolan, 1991:22); a calculation for households lacking any bank account is not available.

Secondly, it is more common in Ireland than in other northern European countries for adult children to remain within the parental household. A large farm sector remains in which household finances are tied to patterns of farm transfer at the point of inheritance. More generally, the difficult economic climate of the late 1980s served to postpone processes of household formation among young people. When combined with the distinctive age structure of the Irish population, the result is a large proportion of households containing three generations, adult siblings living with one parent, and/or several married couples.[9]

Thirdly, in a substantial proportion of Irish households the parents, adult children, or siblings of the principal income earner have an independent source of income. Previous studies have focused on conventional nuclear families: husbands and wives with dependent children. The 1987 ESRI Survey of Income Distribution, Poverty and Usage of State Services has identified a wider range of situations in which adult children, for example, are major contributors to household income. An exclusive focus on spouses when classifying a household in terms of its financial management system will be overly blunt in cases where neither the role of household manager or of principal earner is filled by one of the spouses. In the typical household, the principal income earner is also the owner or renter of the house. There is a significant minority of Irish households to which this does not apply: in 15 per cent of Irish households the household head is the owner/tenant but not the principal economic supporter; that anomaly pertains in 22 per cent of farm households (CSO, 1989: Table 2).

In addition to being appropriate to the Irish context, our classifications need to capture whatever variation exists in financial management among low income households. Most previous research has focused on small numbers of households and removed complications by selecting either only nuclear families with dependent children or particular segments of the population, such as two-income middle class families. As noted, one parent families with adult children and married couples living with one spouse's parents are among the household types so excluded. A focus on families in poverty, and those relying primarily on social welfare for income, makes it impossible to avoid such household types.

---

[9]   See Morris (1989:15-18) for one of the few discussions of resource allocation systems in such households.

Further, low income may impose a particular allocation system on families. Essential bills are paid first, leaving no "excess" about which decisions need to be, or can be, taken (Pahl, 1989:140). It is unclear whether existing classifications will reveal variation among poor households. Whether it will be possible to disentangle the effects of income level, income source, and social class is also uncertain.

Given the experience of research conducted elsewhere, viewed through the lens of specifically Irish socio-economic circumstances and social policy concerns, it seems sensible to focus on two main aspects of family finances. First, how much of income is being shared in Irish households? Sharing means that money is set aside for the "common good" rather than retained by individual earners. Secondly, how is the responsibility for making expenditure decisions divided in Irish households? Treating these as distinct, but related, dimensions of family financial management is sensible given what other studies have found. This also plays to the strengths of the data available to us, which has extensive detail on individual incomes and contributions to household expenses and about who decides on what type of expenditure. Where there is one earner and all of the income is shared, the tendency will be for one household member to take responsibility for day to day management. Where both spouses have an independent income, the possible ways for dividing expenditure responsibility tend to proliferate. Generally, the higher the income and the more equal the income of the spouses where both are income recipients, the wider the range of options available to families for managing their finances. Poverty and low income tend to close off options for how family finances are organised, making it difficult for household members to settle on a system that meets their needs and preferences.

1.5 A Look Ahead

This study is concerned with establishing how much income is shared by members of Irish households, how husbands and wives divide responsibility for expenditure in those households, and the amount of consensus and equality between spouses in the arena of financial decision-making. Chapter 8 states what can be concluded about financial management in Irish households based on a survey carried out in 1989. The raw material for drawing those conclusions is presented in this report in the following manner: Chapter 2 describes the data source; Chapter 3 deals with the extent of income sharing and the division of responsibility for expenditure. Chapter

4 looks at the degree of consensus between spouses on financial matters, the degree of equality between spouses in personal expenditure money and recreational opportunities, and elaborates on the distinction between control and management of family finances. Chapter 5 provides an analysis of the socio-economic factors that affect the extent of income sharing and that shape financial management systems. Chapter 6 considers the impact of income sharing and financial management systems on consensus in family financial decisions, access to personal money and leisure, and levels of psychological distress for husbands and wives. Chapter 7 looks in greater detail at the economic status of women. Particular consideration is given to the significance of Child Benefit and the situation of lone parent families. Finally, conclusions and their implications are presented in Chapter 8.

These diverse topics will relate to the assumptions that are made about what occurs within Irish families and the nature of the interrelationships between such factors as income level, method of financial management, and equality of material well-being within families. The resulting portrait is incomplete and preliminary, but is grounded in the experience of a substantial number of Irish households.

CHAPTER TWO

Data Sources and Measurement

2. Introduction

The report is based on the responses provided by the adult members of the 967 Irish households in a nationwide survey carried out in 1989. This chapter describes the main features of the resulting data, offers guidance as to how to interpret the findings, and introduces the main variables measuring income sharing and division of expenditure responsibility. A more extensive and technical description of how the households were selected and the structure of the survey instruments can be found in Williams and Whelan (1994).

2.1 The Sample

The households participating in the survey come from the second round of the Economic and Social Research Institute's (ESRI) *Lifestyles and Poverty* research programme. The first round of interviews was conducted in the Spring of 1987 and the main findings reported in Callan et al (1988, 1989). Detailed information was collected from all persons aged 15 years and over who had left full-time education, from a target sample of 5,165 households. A multi-stage clustered sampling procedure, based on the electoral register, selected households for the target sample (for details, see Whelan, 1979). This gives each individual on the electoral register an equal probability of selection. The Phase 1 effective sample was subsequently reweighted to eliminate potential bias arising from non-random failures to respond, thus correcting for differences in difficulty of contacting and willingness to participate by occupation, location, or household size. Completed questionnaires were secured from 3,286 households, an effective sample response rate of 64 per cent. This is a high response rate for a detailed survey enquiring about such sensitive and complex issues as income, wealth, and financial well-being.[1]

The second wave of the *Lifestyles and Poverty* survey was undertaken in the Spring of 1989. The data collected in that round forms the core of this report. Funding constraints made it impossible to return to all of the households that responded in the first phase. Instead, it was only possible to reinterview a sub-sample of those households. For Phase 2, therefore, a total target sample of 1,284 households was selected, approximately 40 per cent of the effective Phase 1 sample. Households from the Phase 1 effective sample

---

[1] The *Household Budget Survey*, 1987, for example, had a response rate of approximately 57 per cent. It should be noted that this survey involved respondents maintaining a detailed expenditure diary over a two-week period.

were stratified by income quartile. Because the basic purpose of the research programme was to measure the extent and nature of poverty and to understand the processes underlying its perpetuation, all of those households which were in the lowest income quartile[2] in Phase 1 were included. A random sample of 500 households drawn from the top three quartiles was also selected. This was to ensure that all those in poverty in Phase 1 were included in the second survey. Sampling variances for that subgroup were also minimised.

The target sample of 1,284 households yielded an effective sample of 924 households. Of these, only 918 had sufficiently detailed information on income to permit meaningful analysis. This represents an overall effective sample rate of 72 per cent, eight points higher than in Phase 1. This higher response rate can be attributed to two factors: (i) the Phase 2 respondents had participated in the first round of the survey and so were familiar with its purpose and content and had demonstrated a prior willingness to participate in such research and (ii) the questionnaires in the second phase were less detailed than in the first.

All household based panel surveys, such as the 1987 and 1989 surveys described, must record and take into account changes to their membership. The logic of such a panel study, that reflects change over time, requires that all new households generated in Ireland by former residents of the original households be included in the Phase 2 target sample. Consequently, as each household in the second round of the survey was interviewed, the current composition was compared to a record of its composition at the time of the first interview. If any member of a household had left over the period and had set up a new household in Ireland, then an interview was sought with that household. This was in addition to the Phase 2 target sample of 1,284 households.

Two hundred newly generated households were identified. Not all of these could be contacted: 77 of the new households had been set up abroad by members of Phase 1 households who had emigrated. As such they no longer constituted a valid component of the population of Irish households and

---

[2]   A quartile is where the population is ranked from those on the lowest income to those on the highest income and then divided into four groups, containing the same number in each group. Thus the lowest income quartile is the quarter of the population whose incomes are lowest.

could be safely disregarded without consequences for the representativeness of the effective sample; no address could be found for a further 24 of the newly generated households. Of the remaining 99 households, 33 were either never available or refused to co-operate and 16 referred to individuals who had been resident in a panel household in Phase 1 but who, by Phase 2, had moved to an institution. Successful interviews were completed with 50 newly generated households. One new household was excluded from the sample for analysis due to incomplete information on income.

As a result, the total effective sample from the second stage of the *Lifestyles and Poverty* Research programme was 967: 918 households that "survived" from the first round of interviewing in 1987 and 49 newly generated households.

Attention in this chapter focuses on some of the limitations that should be kept in mind when reading the report. First, although this is one of the larger studies of financial management systems within households, as measured by the number of participating households, it is still small in relation to the differences that exist among households, particularly those at the bottom of the income distribution.

Secondly, financial allocation is but one of many topics examined in the overall survey, Phase 2 of the ESRI Panel on *Lifestyles, Income and Utilization of State Services*. Only a section of the questionnaire was devoted to the specific issue of household financial management, although many other questions, such as those describing individual and household income, are highly pertinent to this report. Given the sensitive nature of the subject matter, ie family finances, the information is not complete for all families, reducing the numbers on which we can report findings. It should be stressed, however, that the level of response to both phases was high and compares favourably to what is achieved in surveys of this nature (Callan, Nolan *et al*, 1989: Chapter 4; Williams and Whelan, 1994).

Thirdly, the Phase 2 households represent a sub-sample of the original households participating in the ESRI panel study. That sub-sample was selected on a disproportionate basis and it is therefore necessary to reweight the data to obtain results that are representative of the national population. This was most in evidence when looking at how families differ by, say, social class or income level. Because of the reweighting the margin of error can be assumed to be large around estimates of what proportion of Irish households correspond to a specific set of characteristics. However, we have ample grounds for claiming that the reweighted sample is an accurate guide to the income levels, social welfare receipts, and labour force status of Irish households. By implication, the sample is an accurate guide to other household characteristics (Callan, Nolan *et al*, 1989: Chapter 4; Williams and Whelan, 1994). This is further discussed later in the chapter.

Fourthly, the report focuses on families where both spouses are resident, and responded to the survey. This accounts for some 67 per cent of all households; 625 couples and their families. There are too few examples of other family or household situations, eg where a widow or widower lives with unmarried adult children or where siblings share a household, to study their financial arrangements.

In the chapters that follow, the analyses and interpretations tend to remain well within the bounds of what can be stated with confidence using the survey data. The more sceptical and statistically adept reader may wish to consult Appendix A to make up their own mind as to the weight of evidence for the conclusions that are drawn. Details are offered on the linkage between the two rounds of surveys and the reweighting, and a partial validation of the resulting estimates is undertaken.

2.2. The Questionnaires

In the first phase of the *Lifestyles and Poverty* research programme a highly detailed and intensive set of questions was asked of the head of the household. This sought to collect *household* level information on household composition: age, sex, marital status, level of educational attainment, labour force status of all household members, extent of utilisation of the health services by each household member throughout the year prior to interview, number and type of rooms in the accommodation, details on the nature of tenure, expenditure on household utilities such as electricity, gas, telephone, etc and ownership of motor vehicles and other major consumer items. In addition to this household questionnaire a personal questionnaire was administered to each household member aged 15 years and over (including the household head) who was not in full-time education. This *individual* questionnaire was also detailed, and collected information on, among many other matters: income and financial status; labour market experience and current employment status; attitudes to social issues relating to poverty and the poor; attitudes to the Social Welfare system; lifestyle; access to social and family support networks and indicators of psychological stress levels. A further detailed survey form was administered to each farmer in the panel and covered: output and activity levels; costs; capital, stock, plant etc. (For a detailed description of the contents of the Phase 1 questionnaires see Callan et al 1989: section 4.6).

Phase 2 of the *Lifestyles and Poverty* research programme aimed to specifically address two previously uninvestigated aspects of poverty in Ireland (a) the dynamics of poverty and (b) the subject of this report, the internal allocation and management of resources within the household. The questionnaire used for Phase 2 therefore contains sections concerning decision-taking within the household, household management and budgetary systems, as well as the current income position, labour market experiences, and compositional changes over the study period.

Resource constraints associated with Phase 2 did not allow us to reinterview each household member aged 15 years and over as had been done in Phase 1. In the second round of interviewing it was only feasible to administer a household-related questionnaire to the head of household, along with individual questionnaires to the head of household and to the spouse of the head of household (where appropriate). A set of questions was asked of both spouses to allow investigation of the decision-making processes in the household, and the level of agreement between the spouses as to how financial decisions were made.

The household-specific questionnaire used for interview with the head of household was divided into three sections:

(a) Characteristics of household members, including their marital status, labour force status, level of educational attainment and occupation, as well as their relationship to the head of household.

(b) Usage of the health service by each household member in the twelve months preceding interview.

(c) Amount and source of the current income of all household members other than household head and spouse (where relevant). This was collected in a sufficiently detailed fashion to allow it to be disaggregated into the main subheadings of wage, farm, self

employment, earned income, social welfare income, State
employment, training schemes and "other sources" such as private
retirement pensions, dividends, interest, rent, etc.[3]

The personal interview with heads of household and spouses were broadly
similar in structure and content and collected details on five main areas as
follows:

(a) Opinions on changes in the household's own economic circumstances
over the study period (ie 1987 to 1989) and on their perceptions of the
level of income necessary to sustain their family at various standards of
living. This section also collected details on the availability to the
household of a wide range of goods and services and on whether a
lack of any of these was imposed by financial constraints or was a
reflection of household preferences.

(b) Labour market experiences and status changes over the study period.

(c) Sources and amounts of income. This involved collecting detailed
information on income from employment, self employment, farming,
social welfare transfers including Supplementary Welfare Allowance
and Family Income Supplement, "other sources" such as retirement
pensions, regular allowances from outside the household, annuities,
trusts, rental income, etc.

(d) Style of living indicators. This involved looking at social and family
networks; ways of handling the household's finances, including
contributions made by all members in multi-earner households;
allowances for personal discretional expenditure; and ways of coping
with unforeseen bills and financial problems.

(e) Health and contact. This collected information on the physical and

---

[3]   It is obvious that collecting information from the head of household on the
income of other household members may introduce some inaccuracy to the figure
derived for total household income. It should be noted, however, that detailed
information on their own income was provided by the head of household and
spouse (where relevant) in separate questionnaires. In Phase 1, where income
details were collected from all members individually, an average of 21 per cent of
household income was accounted for by household membares other than the two
spouses; the comparable figure in Phase 2 is 17 per cent.

psychological well-being of household members using standard sets of questions to measure levels of psychological distress and feelings of powerlessness or fatalism. Frequency of contact with friends and relatives was also asked.

2.3 Measuring Household Disposable Income

The household disposable income concept used in the second phase of the *Lifestyles and Poverty Survey* was, as far as possible, comparable to that used by the Central Statistics Office (CSO) in the *Household Budget Survey* and also in the first phase of the *Lifestyles and Poverty* research programme. Where feasible, information on income was collected on the basis of the most recent current pay period (eg, weekly, fortnightly, monthly). In line with CSO practice no adjustments were made for temporary increases or decreases in the most recent pay figure. For farmer and self-employed income it was necessary to take a longer term perspective in the accounting period used.

The disposable income concept used throughout this report includes all earned income from the following sources: employment; self-employment; farming; State training employment schemes; interest and dividends from deposit accounts, stocks, shares, etc; occupational pensions, rental income; annuities, trusts or covenants; strike or sick pay; and other receipts such as private income continuance or sickness insurance, wet-time payments, etc. Disposable income also includes all transfers through the social welfare system including Child Benefit, Supplementary Welfare Allowance and Family Income Support, educational grants/ scholarships, and private transfers, eg, from family members living apart from the household.

The only difference between ESRI and CSO coverage of income components is the latter's inclusion of an imputed value for free meals, food, and fuel received from an employer. Account was taken of these items by the CSO by adding their imputed value to its "other direct income" subheading, along with such items as annuities, trusts and covenants, and trade union sick or strike pay. (For details see *Household Budget Survey 1987*: Vol 1, Appendix 3). This, however, constitutes a minute element to total disposable income and does not affect comparability of the CSO and ESRI income estimates.

The only deductions from gross income taken into account by the disposable income concept are compulsory income tax and PRSI payments. Other deductions at source such as superannuation, life insurance premia, VHI payments, etc are deemed to be disposable income, again in line with CSO practice.

The disposable income figure used for the self-employed is after tax profit for the most recent 12 month period available once all salaries and wages paid to employees and other expenses have been deducted. This is based entirely on disposable *cash* income. No account is taken of either indirect taxation or non-cash social services in areas such as health, education and housing.

2.4 Interpreting the Data

A few points can be made to offer some guidance on how to interpret the findings presented in this report. Some of the questions that form the basis of this report were asked of both spouses and some were asked only of the "household manager", as designated by the household members.[4] Where questions were asked of both spouses, the interviews were undertaken separately. Separate interviews did not in all cases entail the absence of the other spouse from the room during the interview. Candour may have been somewhat inhibited by the other spouse's presence. However, the sheer length of the survey, the wide range of questions being asked, some differences in the survey format used for husbands and wives all limit the degree to which one spouse's responses could have affected those given by the other. Further, many of the key questions were answered from cards containing a set of options that were handed to the person being interviewed.

One major strand of questions presented issues of interpretation because it was asked of only one household member. The household manager was asked to describe family financial arrangements. In multi-earner households, the household manager provided the interviewer with the usual contribution

---

[4] In practice, for married couples, the instructions lead to the wife being treated as the household manager and the primary source for information on family finances, although in multi-earner households the person answering that set of questions was asked to designate the "household manager", defined as "the one who makes most of the decisions about day-to-day spending". Although this practice can be justified as a pragmatic stance for conducting an initial national survey on the topic, future studies should (a) ensure that both spouses respond to the full set of questions without preconceptions as to their roles in family finances and (b) that interviews with spouses are always completed separately.

each earner makes to household expenses and whether that contribution was more than 90 per cent of the person's net income. The household manager also indicated which household member took responsibility for each of ten expenditure items. Here, the interview structure sought to obtain information from the person best placed to respond accurately. In a perfect survey research world, unconstrained by respondent's time or by other areas of inquiry to be covered in the interview or by budgets, a more comprehensive set of answers would be sought. In this instance, however, information on contributions to household expenses were provided by the household manager and income details, either directly by the earner in the case of the head of household and household manager, or indirectly by the head of household for all other earners.

Finally, because of the sampling methodology followed, the Phase 2 data differ in some respects from a conventional panel survey. The data can be interpreted in a similar manner to a cross-sectional survey undertaken in 1987, in which a wide range of prospective data on future changes over the next two years in income levels, labour market experience, household composition were collected. The characteristics reported, therefore, are not strictly speaking those of the 1987 population per se, but rather the 1989 characteristics of the surviving 1987 population of households. Although the methodological point is important in its implications for statistical inference using the Phase 2 data, in practice, the differences between the figures presented in this report and what would be found for the 1989 population in its totality are likely to be slight. Differences are minimised by the inclusion of the new households entering the system over the period 1987 to 1989, at the cost, however, of further complicating the reweighting of the households in order to be representative.

CHAPTER THREE

Financial Management in Irish Households

3. Introduction

This chapter takes two essential steps toward an analysis of what the survey data can tell us abut family financial management in Irish households. The first step is to capture the most salient features of how allocation decisions are made in Irish families. The second step is to look at how the prevalence of various types of allocation systems compare to what research has identified in other countries. Those two steps are dependent, however, on an understanding of what is available for households to allocate internally, ie the composition of disposable household income.

3.1 The Composition of Disposable Household Income

On average, households that include a married couple have a weekly disposable income of £244.78 (1989). Only half of that money (53 per cent) is attributable to the husband's employment or self-employment. If all earners are included, employment accounts for 75 per cent of household disposable income. The remainder consists of social welfare payments (16 per cent), occupational pensions and investment income (7 per cent) and Child Benefit (3 per cent). A more detailed profile of household income is provided in Table 3.1 which looks at two facets of its composition: (a) the percentage that each type of income represents of the total household average income and (b) the percentage of households receiving income from that source. Thus, Child Benefit payments accrue to 70 per cent of the households and, on average, represent 3 per cent of their average disposable incomes.

For the purposes of this study, several features of household income are particularly noteworthy. Social welfare payments are both widespread and a significant component of income. In the spring of 1989, 37 per cent of husbands and 9 per cent of wives received a social welfare payment (including old age pensions). In 10 per cent of the households, a member other than the husband or the wife was a social welfare recipient. Nearly two-thirds of the husbands have income from employment or self-employment, as do nearly one-quarter of wives. Household members other than the husband or wife had an earned income in nearly one-fifth (18 per cent) of households. Income in the form of investments' interest accrues to one-third of the husbands and over one-fifth of the wives (22 per cent). In terms of financial management, therefore, there is a substantial number of multiple earner households, as well as a smaller, but still significant, number of households in which the wife has a bank account or other investment that earns interest.[1]

Table 3.1 The Average Composition of Household Disposable Income[*]

Income Source	Share in Total Disposable Household Income	Percentage of Households with Income from Source
	Per Cent	Per Cent
Husband's	**69.3**	
Employment	52.8	65.9
Social Welfare	11.5	37.4
Pension	3.4	9.6
Investments	1.6	33.7
Wife's	**14.0**	
Employment	10.8	24.1
Social Welfare	1.9	8.9
Pension	0.2	1.1
Investments	1.1	21.8
Other Member's	**14.0**	
Employment	11.4	18.3
Social Welfare	2.2	10.4
Pension/ Investments	0.4	5.6
Child Benefit	**2.6**	**70.0**
Total	**100.0** (N=625)	

* This table is based on the average weekly disposable income of a married couple (£244.78)

[1] Averages indicate the central tendency in a distribution of scores or values and standard deviations indicate how closely the households are clustered around that central point. The average figures presented here tend to be associated with large standard deviations. This follows, in part, from the fact that the households are being included in the calculation even if they do not receive income from that source. So while the households receive on average £26.36 weekly from wives' employment, if consideration is restricted to the 150 households in which the wife is employed (roughly one out of every four households), the average rises to the more considerable £109.87 (with a standard deviation of 61.5). Even the average that is most inclusive, however, that for total household disposable income, has a large standard deviation relative to the average. As a rule of thumb, where standard deviations exceed more than half of an average, there is quite a substantial degree of spread around the average and it consequently lacks precision.

3.2 Income Sharing in Irish Families

Some form of income sharing can be found in the overwhelming majority of Irish families, with one or more household members paying an allowance or contributing to a household "kitty" in 85 per cent of families. In the average family, household members share an estimated 55 per cent of their incomes. The weekly grocery bill (defined as "food and household essentials") accounts, on average, for 59 per cent of the total amount that is being shared.

The averages are based on the 625 households in which a married couple is present and both spouses were interviewed. The average amount being shared is estimated by taking the total amount contributed to household expenses by *all* household members (as reported by the household manager) and dividing it by the total income of *all* members of the household. Similarly, the extent to which shared income is being used for essentials is calculated by dividing the amount reported as typically spent for that purpose weekly by the typical amount of income that is shared.[2]

While it is evident that sharing is significant in its prevalence and the amount of money involved, households obviously differ in how they manage the money that is shared. The next step taken in this chapter is therefore to

---

[2] The standard deviation for both average percentages is 0.33 and for average amount shared is £102. Where households do not share income, this average is not relevant, and the average is based on the 494 income sharing households reporting full information. Looking at median values for the percentages and amount contributed, a measure of the typical value that is less susceptible to influence by extreme scores, gives much the same result. Medians measure the "central" or typical value by indicating where exactly one half of the households report a smaller value and one half a larger value. For the percentage of income being shared, the median is 57 per cent, the median grocery bill as a percentage of what is shared is 54 per cent, and the median amount shared is £120 weekly. The inter-quartile range is a conventional way to describe variation in such circumstances. In this study, households were ranked from lowest to highest on each of the three variables and the value at the 25th and 75th percentiles were established. For example, at the 25th percentile 32 per cent of income is shared, indicating that one of every four households has a percentage lower than that.

	25th Percentile Value	75th Percentile Value	Range
% Shared	32	88	56
% on Groceries	36	75	39
Amount Shared	£69	£192	123

devise ways of classifying households in terms of how spouses divide responsibilities for expenditure.

3.3 Dividing Expenditure Responsibilities

The household manager was asked a series of questions designed to classify the nature of the financial management system being used. In doing so, those interviewed were directed into one of three strands of linked questions depending on household composition and the number of household members with their own incomes. The first strand was devised for households with only one resident adult. This applies to 20 per cent of all the households. Such households are not considered in this chapter, as, by definition, they do not include married couples and, however pressing their financial problems, their situations provide little scope for variation in how financial decisions are made. The risk of poverty faced by one adult households with dependent children is considered in Chapter 7.

Where two or more adults were present, separate strands of questions inquired about financial management in one-earner and two-earner households. This recognizes the far greater potential for variation in households where either both spouses or one spouse *and* other household members have independent incomes. Of households including a married couple (and where one of them is designated the "head of household"), 300 out of 625 have one earner. Earnings are defined as any form of recurrent income. Four possible ways of organising household finances were shown to the household manager in one-earner households. The descriptions selected as describing their arrangements and the percentage selecting each choice can be found in Figure 3.1. Most of the one-earner households report managing their finances using a method approximating the "whole wage" system. Overwhelmingly, one-earner households choose the "whole wage" system with wife control: 74 per cent give that response, a representation equivalent to 37 per cent of all households with married couples. The whole wage system with husband control, in which the main earner retains his income and pays all bills, applies to about 5 per cent of all one-earner households (2 per cent of married couples). The remaining one-earner households report using an "allowance system", either to cover all expenses (12 per cent of one-earner households; 6 per cent of married couples) or "most household expenses" (9 per cent of one-earner households; 5 per cent of married couples).

Household managers were asked to fit their way of making financial decisions into one of the four possibilities. The infrequency of alternatives to the whole wage system with wife control, particularly relative to what has been found in England, suggests two tentative implications. One is that the factors that traditionally promoted the use of whole wage and allowance systems are strongly present in one-earner Irish households. A second is that one-earner Irish households tend, on average, to have limited scope for more complex arrangements, although it is possible that such exist and represent variants of the "allowance system".

Figure 3.1 Financial Management Systems : One-Earner Households

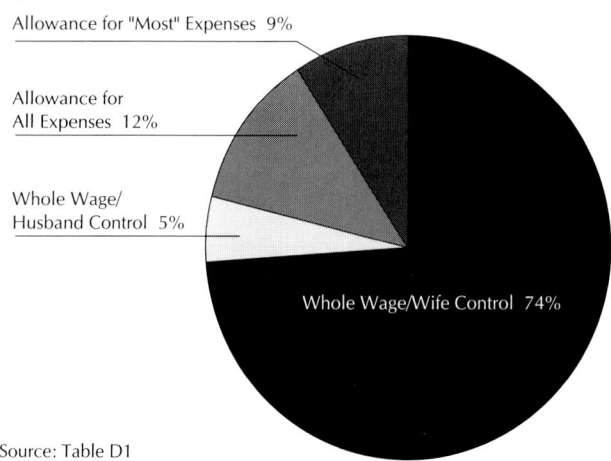

Allowance for "Most" Expenses 9%

Allowance for
All Expenses 12%

Whole Wage/
Husband Control 5%

Whole Wage/Wife Control 74%

Source: Table D1

Greater diversity can be anticipated in households where two or more members have regular sources of income. Household managers in such situations were asked "the usual weekly contribution to household expenses" by each earner. Details on income were available separately for each contributor. Information on the contributions and incomes of the husband, wife, and other household members were combined to create six categories for describing financial management in multi-earner households. The main criterion is the degree to which the main income earner shares his or her income as part of a general household "kitty". Another criterion is whether both spouses have independent sources of income.[3]

---

[3] Responses provided in the financial allocation section of the surveys from 28 households were incomplete and it is not possible to classify them other than as "multi-earner" households.

Figure 3.2 shows the financial management systems in operation and their relative frequency. Six methods of sharing income can be identified, forming systems 5 to 10 in the figure. In systems 5 and 6, only one spouse has a regular income of £20 per week or greater.[4] These divide almost exactly into those where the contribution to household expenses amounts to more than three-quarters of the main earner's income (System 5) and those where the contribution is less (System 6). Combined, these systems account for 37 per cent of all multi-earner households and 20 per cent of all married couples. In effect, System 5 is similar to the whole wage system in one-earner households and System 6 to the allowance system.

The diversity likely within multi-earner households is most evident in System 7, in which both spouses have an income and make equal contributions to a general housekeeping budget. This corresponds to a pooled management system (describing 13 per cent of multi-earner households; 7 per cent of married couples). System 8, which describes 18 per cent of multi-earner households and 9 per cent of married couples, also entails contributions from both spouses and the amount is consistently greater than 75 per cent of their individual incomes. For most purposes, it can be regarded as similar to the households under System 7. The practice of making equal contributions, however, seems sufficiently distinct to justify treating such households as practising a special type of income pooling.

Lesser degrees of pooling are represented in systems 9 and 10. In system 9, the main earner contributes more than three-quarters of their income and the other spouse less than that proportion of their income. This represents 14 per cent of multi-earner households and 7 per cent of married couples. Finally, in system 10 neither spouse, both of whom have independent incomes of more than £20 weekly, contributes more than three-quarters of their income to a common kitty. A non-pooled arrangement of this nature prevails in the same percentage of households as does the previous system.

---

[4] That restriction is imposed to eliminate from these categories households in which the income being shared is typically in the form of bank interest, which tends to be paid annually or semi-annually, or intermittent earnings that are a minor component of total household income.

Figure 3.2 Financial Management Systems in Ireland: Married Couples

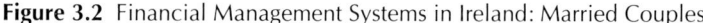

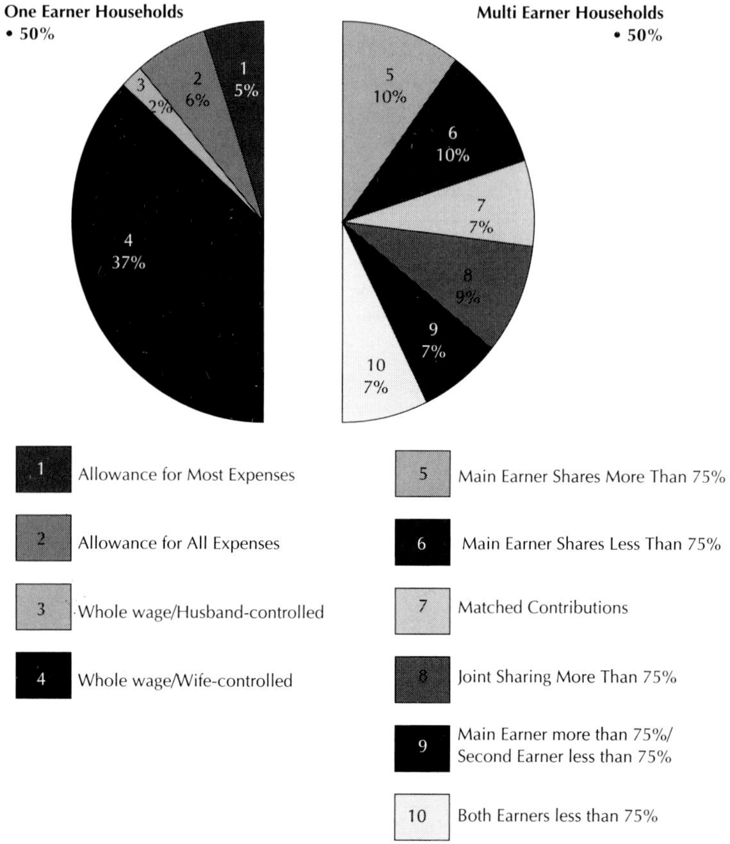
One Earner Households
• 50%
Multi Earner Households
• 50%
1
5%
2
6%
3
2%
4
37%
5
10%
6
10%
7
7%
8
9%
9
7%
10
7%
1 Allowance for Most Expenses
2 Allowance for All Expenses
3 Whole wage/Husband-controlled
4 Whole wage/Wife-controlled
5 Main Earner Shares More Than 75%
6 Main Earner Shares Less Than 75%
7 Matched Contributions
8 Joint Sharing More Than 75%
9 Main Earner more than 75%/ Second Earner less than 75%
10 Both Earners less than 75%

Source: Table D2

Ten distinct management systems may accurately reflect the variety of ways in which households manage their finances, but such a classification is cumbersome in terms of analysis and interpretation. Some simplification can be introduced, however, by giving priority to the extent of sharing. Systems 5, 7 and 8 tend toward the "whole wage" approach in single earner households, while systems 6, 9 and 10 are similar to the principle underlying the allowance system.

A summary assessment can be offered of the amount of sharing by husbands and wives in families where both are at work. In such households, the median contribution of husbands is 69 per cent of their earnings and the median contribution of wives is 78 per cent.[5] There is no apparent difference in the rate at which husbands contribute from their incomes between households where wives are employed and households where the other household members, but not the wife, are at work.

Although the ten categories isolate some interesting features of financial management in Irish households, as a classification scheme they are deficient on several grounds. One is that one-earner households are necessarily treated as distinct from multi-earner households, a consequence of questionnaire design. A second is that too many management systems are identified to enable relatively straightforward interpretation. This leads us to look to who takes direct responsibility for specific items of expenditure as our principal measure of financial management.

3.4 Spheres of Expenditures and Financial Management

Irish families share incomes in a considerable variety of ways. Does this lead to a reduction in the traditional gender-based division of responsibilities for household management? One basis for answering that question is to look at which spouse takes responsibility for specific areas of expenditure. The designated "household manager" in each household was asked: *How are the following items usually paid for?* with ten specific items listed. Figure 3.3 lists the items and the percentage of "managers" selecting each response.[6] Generally, the "household manager" is the wife and the "main earner" is the husband and the table should be interpreted on this assumption.

---

[5] The mean or average gives much the same result as the centre of the distribution, but with a less dramatic difference between husbands and wives. Based on 129 households in which full information is available for both spouses the means and standard deviations (shown in parentheses) are 65 per cent (27) for husbands and 71 per cent (27) for wives. Medians, averages, and quartile values are virtually identical for husbands' contributions in the 169 households in which a household member other than the spouse has an income. This refers to the *distribution* of percentages being contributed.

[6] The choices cover a range of recurrent and essential demands, and differentiate between child-specific, wife-specific, and husband-specific expenses. However, future research should supplement this with questions on who decides on the timing and choice of major consumer purchases, such as automobiles or television sets.

The responses given to these questions on expenditure responsibility offer a basis for determining the kinds of allocation systems being used by Irish families. The following classification was developed specifically to describe the situation among Irish married couples in 1989:[7]

Whole Wage System (One person management)	One household member, usually the wife, is responsible for all routine purchases
Allowance System (Main Earner Control)	The main earner, usually the husband, is responsible for all routine purchases
Joint Management	Some routine purchases made from allowance or kitty; other purchases made directly by main earner; and,
Independent Management	Routine purchases by both spouses from their own incomes and from a joint kitty

In most households, the wife takes responsibility for purchasing food and providing for children's needs from the household "kitty" or from an allowance. Women with incomes take responsibility for children's clothing and school expenses, as well as their own clothing. The clearest distinction is in major recurring bills for housing and fuel, which are paid directly by the main earner in between a fifth and a third of households. Still, for all expenditure items the typical situation which describes more than half of the married couples, is for the wife to be responsible, relying on either an allowance or a joint "kitty" that she manages. Clearly, traditional divisions of labour within the family are paralleled in divisions of responsibility for expenditure spheres.

---

[7] There are some difficulties in terminology. While most Irish households practice a form of financial management approximating either the whole wage or allowance systems, the labels do not adequately describe the dynamics of what is taking place. An alternative set of categories based on responsibility can be used: (a) one person management; (b) main earner control; (c) joint management; and (d) independent management. The measure of expenditure spheres is offered as a new classification of what Pahl (1989) and others refer to as the household's allocation system.

Figure 3.3 Spheres of Expenditure Responsibility:
How are these items usually paid for?

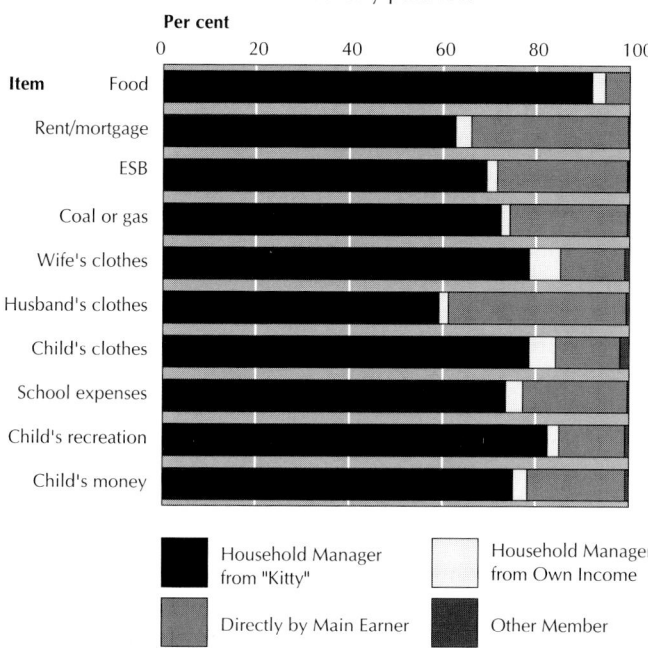

Source: Table D3

When the responses given to the ten expenditure items are used simultaneously to describe households, two main types emerge. In nearly one-half (48 per cent), *all* expenses are paid for by the household manager from an allowance or "kitty", representing clear instances of wife management. A second substantial group of households (38 per cent) shares expenditure responsibility so that some items are purchased by the household manager from an allowance or "kitty", some by the household manager from (usually her) income, and some directly by the main income earner. Spouses in these households are pooling parts of their incomes and dividing responsibilities according to expenditure spheres. Typically, this entails wives taking responsibility for daily essentials and the needs of children, and husbands assuming responsibility for paying weekly or monthly bills for housing and utilities.

41

Two smaller groups of households can also be identified. A division of expenditure into spheres of responsibility without a pooling of incomes is evident in about one tenth of households with a married couple. In these households, all expenses are paid for either directly by the main earner or directly by the household manager out of their own income. There are also households in which the main earner pays directly for all expenses, but these account for less than one out of every twenty households (4.5 per cent).[8]

On balance, although full-fledged whole wage management/wife control is the most common arrangement and expenditure spheres tend to be divided to fit traditional gender roles, there is evidence that within a substantial proportion of Irish families more complex arrangements for sharing of incomes and expenditure responsibilities exist.

If the results are viewed in the light of the discussion in Chapter 1, the most striking finding is that the prevalence of various types of financial management systems in Ireland differs considerably from what is reported in British studies. In the mid-1980s, whole wage systems were scarce in Britain, being present in about one out of every six households. Allowance-based systems were more common, but represented only one out of every four households. Half of British households used a shared management system, and one out of twelve practiced independent management (Pahl, 1983: pp 245-9). The results of the 1989 Phase 2 survey present a strikingly different pattern for Irish households. Most one-earner Irish households still follow a whole wage system. Multi-earner households tend toward an allowance-based system. Some more complex systems of financial management are also evident. In 14 per cent of Irish multi-earner households (7 per cent of all households), the spouses contribute equal amounts for common use.

If one-earner and multi-earner households are combined, the division of expenditure responsibilities leads to the following classification of Irish households in 1989: one half use one person management (equivalent to whole wage management, wife control); a further 5 per cent represent main earner control (equivalent to the allowance system, husband control); nearly one in four households use joint (or shared) management in the form of a "kitty" or allowance that is supplemented by direct purchase of some

---

[8]   The unweighted number of households in this category is larger than its percentage share of the weighted sample suggests. As a result, there is sufficient scope for further analysis of the characteristics of the households in this category.

essential items by the main earner; and in one household in ten independent management prevails. Independent management means that both spouses purchase some items directly out of their own incomes and, usually, others from a pooled household "kitty".

On balance, the persistence of traditional financial management practices in Ireland is the main theme that emerges: full-fledged wife management is the most common arrangement and expenditure spheres, when divided, tend to be allocated to fit traditional gender roles. There appears, however, to be sufficient scope within two earner families to permit a substantial proportion of families to forge more complex arrangements that exhibit joint or independent financial decision-making. Insight into these arrangements is restricted in this study by the absence in the survey data of information on banking practices and the use of a classification for financial management systems that varies from that used in British studies.

3.5 Conclusion

Income sharing is the norm in Irish households. The amount being shared, however, differs considerably. The typical amount is just over one half of all household income. There is evidence for frequent use of both whole wage or allowance systems in single earner households, but where both spouses have an income or adult children are present, a variety of situations need to be distinguished. It is difficult to apply a simple classification of household finances where there is more than one income earner present.

The division of expenditure responsibilities in Irish families can be described using a more compact set of categories. A substantial proportion of all families are still wife managed, with all routine expenses being paid by the household manager using either an allowance or access to a "kitty". That traditional method of financial management co-exists, however, with a diversity of more complex arrangements in which both spouses have identifiable spheres of responsibility.

Several limitations emerge to what we can know with confidence based on the survey data. The main limitation is one encountered by previous researchers, namely that family financial arrangements do not fit into tidy categories. Perhaps between the extremes of very low income, on the one hand, and two earner professional families with separate and (perhaps) joint bank accounts reserved for designated purposes, on the other, similar households can be identified. But they do not describe the situation of the majority of households. One extension to the current research is to explore the boundaries, perhaps unspoken, as to how much which spouse can spend. This would require a more extensive set of questions than could be asked in the space restrictions of the ESRI Panel survey, in which household financial arrangements were but one of many topics investigated.

CHAPTER FOUR

Financial Decisions and Decision-Makers:
A First Look

4. Introduction and Background

This chapter is descriptive, reporting what can be learned about how families make financial decisions from the responses husbands and wives gave in the 1989 survey. Background material relevant to that topic is also considered, such as the relative importance of different sources of income to the households being studied. Generally, the term household, not family, is used for the units whose patterns and structures are being described. Most households, particularly those in which a husband and wife are resident, can reasonably be regarded as constituting a family for our purposes.

Little is known about how Irish families manage their finances. There is evidence associating the whole wage and the allowance systems with Irish urban families and husband control with Irish farm families. Humphreys observed that:

> shopping for the family and even for individual family members is almost exclusively the wife's province ... the husband *generally* gives her his wage, except for a small amount to cover personal expenses, and leaves its administration to her...(1966:41).

This describes the allowance system used by Irish urban families in the 1950s for financial management. The whole wage system had been prevalent in their parents' generation. Among rural migrants to Dublin, there was a switch from husband's responsibility for the family budget to wive's responsibility (Humphreys, 1966:236-7). In middle class urban families, however, wife management was associated with greater husband control, relative to the practice in working class families.

There is scant contemporary evidence to verify or update this depiction of family financial management in Irish households. Daly (1989:27-30) does consider the management and control of family money as it relates to the impact and nature of poverty in Ireland, citing one of the few available small-scale studies, focusing on "very poor" households, found that virtually all budget "very strictly":

> Usually money is first set aside for "fixed bills" such as rent, fuel, debt repayments. Food is then bought from what is left over. Any money to spare after this is quickly absorbed by other necessities. Money is so tight in poor families that clothes and footwear are not normally budgeted for out of weekly income - these are paid for by child benefit, if possible (Daly 1989:28).

The series of questions about family finances asked during Phase 2 (1989) of the ESRI Panel Study, in conjunction with the extensive range of questions on family income, composition, and labour market participation, can begin to flesh out a contemporary picture of how families manage their finances. That picture is further enlarged by the availability of answers by both spouses to many of the evaluative, subjective questions, and to indices that measure the stress and sense of control felt by husbands and wives.

4.1 Financial Circumstances: Assessments by Husbands and Wives

Both spouses were asked to assess their household's economic situation in five questions. This section looks at the responses to these questions and raises the following issues: how much divergence is there between husband and wives? and is there a tendency for wives to be more optimistic or pessimistic than their spouses?

Spouses tend to agree in their description of the recent state of their household's finances, as shown in Table 4.1. Agreement is made likely when a dichotomy is presented and when one of those choices describes acute deprivation. But the level of agreement is also very high when spouses are asked to use a five point scale to describe their financial circumstances. There is a slight, but only slight, tendency for husbands to be the more pessimistic about the household's economic circumstances.

The consistency of agreement between spouses can be expressed as a scale, between zero and five. To construct the scale, the definition of what constitutes disagreement is revised for questions 1 and 5 to avoid small semantic differences in their assessments. In the questions of change in overall financial situation, disagreement means that one spouse claimed an improvement and the other a disimprovement over the last twelve months (disagreements where one said things "stayed the same" and the other perceived a change are not included).[1] In the question on whether "you had to do without things that you feel are necessary", the responses "very often" and "a few times" were combined and opposed to responses of "hardly ever" and "never".

---

[1]   An exception is made where one spouse claims that the financial situation had "stayed the same" while the other claimed that it had either "got much better" or "got much worse".

Table 4.1 Patterns of Agreement and of Pessimism in Financial Assessments

		% Agreement	Pessimistic	
			% Wives	% Husbands
1.	Has your overall financial situation ....? (5 Choices)	63.9	35.2	39.3
2.	Unable to pay mortgage, rent gas or ESB? (yes/no)	94.8	14.5	15.2
3.	Gone into debt to pay mortgage, rent, gas or ESB? (yes/no)	95.2	13.0	13.2
4.	Gone into debt to pay other ordinary living expenses? (yes/no)	94.5	13.5	12.5
5.	Had to do without things that you feel are necessary to pay mortgage, rent, gas or ESB? (5 Choices)	71.9	27.2	28.9

The responses given to the five questions suggest consensus on the household's recent financial situation. The frequency of disagreement is shown in Figure 4.1. Within the limitations of the questions asked, there is a substantial degree of consistency in the assessment husbands and wives make of their financial circumstances. This, of course, leaves little room for differences to emerge in how husbands and wives perceive the extent of the economic problems that they collectively face.

Agreement on who would make a "big" financial decision moves the debate on to consideration of how money is spent, as opposed to the general state of the household finances. Both spouses were asked: "*If an unforeseen medical bill of, say, £100 were to arise, who do you think would decide how to meet it?*".[2] The pattern of responses can be seen in Table 4.2.

---

[2] Most low income households would possess medical cards, which might make the unforeseen medical bill less sensitive as an indicator of who makes non-routine financial decisions in the family. However, it is reasonable to assume that respondents generalised the question to a situation in which the money was needed in cash.

Figure 4.1 Disagreements in Financial Assessments

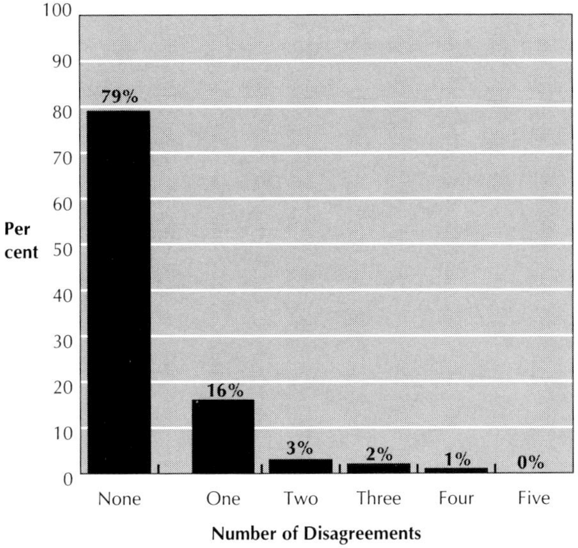

Source: Table D4

Table 4.2 Who Decides on Payment for Major Emergency Expenses*

	Wive's Response			
	Husband	Wife	Joint	Total
Husband's Response				
Husband	10.5	0.9	7.4	**18.7**
Wife	1.0	5.1	2.4	**8.6**
Joint	3.5	3.9	63.5	**71.6**
Total	**14.9**	**9.8**	**73.7**	**100.0** (N=618)

* Each cell contains the percentage of all married couples giving a particular response pattern. Row totals refer to the response by husbands and column totals to the response by wives for each option (eg 18.7 per cent of the husbands answered that they would make the decision; 14.9 per cent of the wives indicated that their husband would make the decision). Row percentages sum across the table and column totals sum down, if some leeway is allowed for rounding errors.

Note: The diagonal from top left to bottom right indicates percentages of couples in which the husband and wife agree in their assessment of who would make such a decision (ie 79.1 per cent).

Overwhelmingly, the couples claim that it would be a joint decision (63 per cent). There is agreement in a further 11 per cent of households that the husband would decide and in 5 per cent that the wife would do so. The spouses in 79 per cent of the households therefore agree on who would make the decision. This leaves a minority of families in which the wife believes that the decision would be made jointly but the husband claims that he would decide (7 per cent of the households) or where the husband says it will be a joint decision and the wife replies that her husband will decide (3 per cent). Disagreements in which each spouse claims that the other would be the one to decide characterise less than 2 per cent of the households.

Apparent consensus also prevails when asked to identify the most likely source of money to meet an emergency bill. Choices include income, savings, cutting back on other expenditure, borrowing from relatives or from a bank or from a money lender. Provision was also made for "other" replies. The likely sources cited by husbands and wives, and the degree to which their answers coincide, can be seen in Table 4.3. There are 49 possible pairings of responses by husbands and wives. The seven possibilities that indicate agreement on what would be the source for the £100 account for 69 per cent of the households.

Table 4.3 Most Likely Source of Money to Meet Emergency Expenditure*

Husband's Response	Wive's Response							Total
	Income	Savings	Cutbacks	Relatives	Bank	Pawnbroker	Other	
				Per cent				
Income	17.6	3.2	2.7	0.2	0.5	-	0.4	**24.6**
Savings	2.4	17.9	2.1	0.2	1.9	-	-	**24.4**
Cutbacks	1.9	0.9	10.9	1.6	2.6	0.1	0.7	**18.8**
Relatives	-	0.5	0.6	9.6	0.8	-	0.1	**11.6**
Bank	0.8	0.3	1.8	1.2	9.8	0.1	0.1	**14.0**
Pawnbroker	-	-	-	0.4	-	0.8	0.1	**1.4**
Other	0.5	0.1	0.9	0.6	0.2	-	2.9	**5.1**
Total	**23.2**	**22.9**	**18.9**	**13.9**	**15.9**	**0.9**	**4.3**	**100** (N=610)

* Each cell contains the percentage of all married couples giving a particular response pattern. Row totals refer to responses by husbands and column totals to the responses by wives to the same question. Rows add across and columns add downward if some leeway is allowed for rounding error.

4.2 Personal Expenditure and Leisure

Do husbands and wives enjoy equal access to personal spending money and to leisure time pursuits? How important is access to an independent source of income for whether wives have money to spend on themselves and opportunities, for say, an afternoon or evening of leisure time?

Money is logically the first topic to consider. Both spouses were asked: *"Most weeks, do you have some money to spend on yourself for your own pleasure or recreation?"* In reply, 76 per cent of husbands and 62 per cent of wives said that they do. Table 4.4 indicates the pattern of response by husbands and wives. This shows a distribution of personal spending money substantially in favour of husbands. In nearly one out of every five households, the husband has personal spending money and the wife does not. The reverse is true in only one household out of twenty.

Do husbands and wives have access to equivalent amounts of money for personal spending? This can be addressed in terms of the absolute amounts being spent and as proportions of personal and household incomes. On average, husbands report having £11.20 weekly for personal spending, while wives report access to £7.66. But these averages are calculated on the basis of all individuals, including those with no personal spending money.[3]

Table 4.4 Access to Personal Spending Money*

Husbands Response	Wive's Response		Total
	Yes	No	
	Per cent		
Yes	56.9	19.9	75.8
No	5.0	19.3	24.2
Total	61.9	38.1	100.0
			(N=613)

* Each cell contains the percentage of all married couples giving a particular response pattern. Row totals refer to the responses by husbands and column totals to the response by wives. Row totals sum across the table and column totals sum down, if some leeway is allowed for rounding errors.
Note: Comparisons here relate to the assessment, by each partner, of their own access. Responses did not allow comparisons of the perceptions of the other partner's access to personal spending money.

---

[3]   For that reason, as well as the general diversity in the amounts of money people have available for personal spending, the standard deviations related to the averages are very substantial (£11.34 for wives and £12.21 for husbands).

Where wives do have access to personal spending money, it is, on average, slightly greater than the amount to which the typical husband has access, £12.56 (standard deviation 12.22) compared to £11.91 (standard deviation 12.25). The large standard deviations suggest that there are several other stories going on simultaneously within this comparison. For example, if we look at the average personal spending money for the husbands of those women who do have personal spending money, the husband's average is greater: £14.62 (standard deviation, 13.11). Other comparisons confirm the consistency of the differential in favour of husbands when like is compared to like. In families where the wife has an independent income, the average personal spending money available to husbands is £14.55 and to the wives £11.48. Focusing on those households in which the wife earns *and* has some personal spending money produces a higher average amount of money (£16.60 per week), but that remains less than the money available to the husband £18.07 per week (applicable to 134 households, in some of which the husband does not report having personal spending money). It is reasonable to conclude at this preliminary stage that husbands tend to have access to some special personal spending money, however modest, at virtually all income levels. Wives are less likely to have access, but when they do, the amounts are apparently likely to come close to, but not to exceed, those of their husbands.

A simple index of equity in access to personal spending money can be constructed by subtracting the wife's personal spending money from that of the husband and dividing the result by the sum of both spouses' personal spending money. This yields a score of +1.0 when the husband has access to all of the money, zero when there are exactly equal shares, and -1.0 when the wife has access to all of the personal spending money.[4] The range of situations in terms of relative spending money in Irish families can be seen in Figure 4.2, which uses histograms to display the concentration of households found at various points along the equity index. The top histogram includes, with a score of zero, those couples that report neither having personal

---

[4] This has an interesting extension. If "m" stands for the husband's spending and "w" for the wive's spending, we can calculate the percentage of the personal spending money that the husband controls at the average score on the equality index. In the present data $(m-w)/(m+w)=0.397$. It follows that: $m-w=0.397m+0.397w$; $0.603m=1.397w$; $m=1.397w/0.603$. At the average value of the equality index, husbands control about 70 per cent of a couple's personal spending money.

Figure 4.2 Personal Spending Money: Equity Between Spouses

(a) All Households

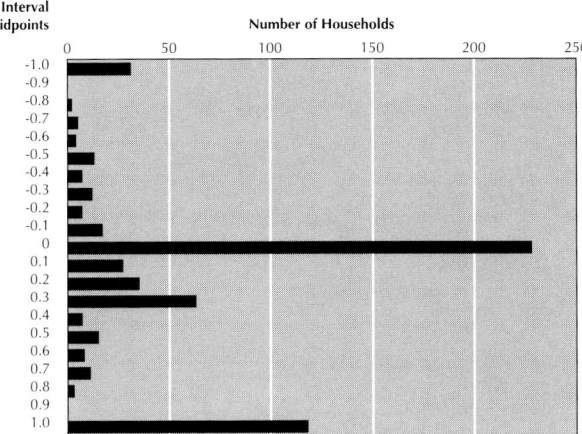

(b) Households in Which at Least One Spouse has Personal Spending Money

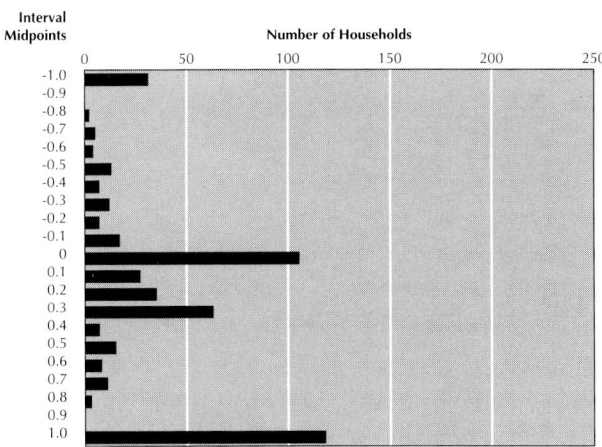

Note: Based on an index that scores 1.0 if the husband controls all the personal spending money; 0 where both spouses have equal amounts of personal spending money; and -1.0 if the wife has access to all of the personal spending money.

spending money. In the bottom histogram, those couples are omitted and a score of zero indicates that the spouses have equal amounts of spending money.

Two strong patterns can be seen in how personal money is distributed. Approximately one-third of all couples have access to equal amounts of spending money. Even when the histogram omits those couples in which neither has access to personal spending money, equality describes nearly one-fifth of the couples. There is a second pattern in which the husband receives the bulk of the personal money. This is anchored by the 118 households in which the husband is the only spouse with personal spending money. However, the typical situation in other households· is for the husband's share to exceed that of the wife.[5]

Access to, and the amount of, personal spending money are important as measures of the distribution of income within a household and as criteria for how husbands and wives fare under different household management systems. The within household distribution of personal spending money is not a simple function of income. Generally, equity is greatest at the two extremes of the income distribution, ie amongst the very poor and the very affluent households. The highest levels of concentration of spending money in the hands of the husband are found in the middle of the income distribution.

As a window on the usually hidden internal financial arrangements of households, the distribution of personal spending money therefore suggests that income levels, on their own, are inadequate for the task of explaining what families experience. There is a clear relationship between the size of household income and the average amount of personal spending money available to the spouses. There are, however, important gender differences. As household income rises, so does the average amount of money husbands have to spend on personal entertainment. The association between household income level and wives' personal spending money is less clear, as consequently, is the difference between husbands and wives in their access to money for their own use. Whether the wife has an independent source of income makes a difference. But even if that is taken into consideration families differ in the relative share spouses have of personal spending money. Figure 4.3 looks at the average amounts reported as available for spending by income quintile, looking separately at husbands, wives, and

---

[5]   The average index of inequality is 0.19.

their combined amounts.[6] In the top quintile of households, 93 per cent of the husbands and 87 per cent of wives have access to personal spending money.

Figure 4.3 Average Amounts of Personal Spending Money by Income Quintile (based on persons reporting some money available)

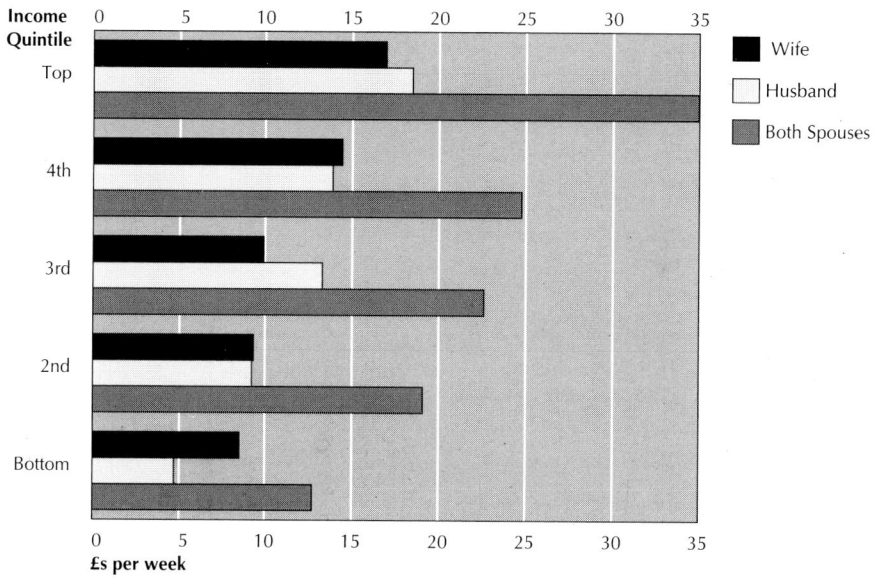

Key: Income quintiles group households on the basis of their total disposable incomes:

Bottom quintile:	Lowest	-	£127.94 per week
2nd quintile:	£127.95	-	£185.94 per week
3rd quintile:	£185.95	-	£247.27 per week
4th quintile:	£247.28	-	£329.42 per week
Top quintile:	£329.43	-	highest per week

Source: Table D5

---

[6] To create the quintiles, households were ranked starting with the one reporting the lowest income through to the household with the highest income. After the first fifth of all households are included, the bottom quintile is defined, containing, by definition, one fifth of all households. To place the percentages into context, the income levels marking the quintile are: bottom (lowest through £127.94 weekly) second (up to £185.94), third (up to £247.27), fourth (up to £329.42), and fifth or top (over £329.42).

The main implication of these averages by household income level is that we are describing a complex phenomenon. In Chapter 6, the complexity will be pursued in terms of the role of labour force participation, allocation mechanisms, and other factors that affect the relative balance of personal spending money.

Another aspect of intra-family equality is the ability to enjoy leisure pursuits and to socialise with one's friends and relations, as seen in Table 4.5. Overall 62 per cent of the husbands and 56 per cent of the wives report that they had *"an afternoon or evening out in the last fortnight, for your entertainment, something that cost money"*. In nearly half of the households with a married couple (47 per cent) both spouses had an afternoon or evening out. Neither spouse reports such an excursion in a further 28 per cent of the married couples. Couples gave the same response, therefore, in three-quarters of the households. Instances where the wife did have time out and the husband did not (9 per cent of couples) were rarer than examples where the husband went out and the wife did not (16 per cent). In summary, there is again a considerable degree of agreement and equity in the pattern of responses, but a layer of inequality in favour of the husband remains.

Table 4.5 Have You Had a Night Out?*

Husbands Response	Wife's Response		Total
	Yes	No	
	Per cent		
Yes	46.8	15.7	**62.4**
No	9.5	28.1	**37.6**
Total	**56.2**	**43.8**	**100.0** (N=621)

* Each cell contains the percentage of all married couples giving a particular response pattern. Row totals refer to responses by husbands and column totals to responses by wives to the same question (eg 62.4 per cent of husbands and 56.2 per cent of wives had a night out in the previous fortnight). Rows add across and columns add downward if some leeway is allowed for rounding error.

Those who claimed not to have had an evening out within the previous fortnight were asked why, being prompted by five possible reasons and given the opportunity to add additional ones. The reasons cited by husbands and wives (respondents were asked to select the most pressing) can be compared in Figure 4.4.

Figure 4.4 Main Reasons for Not Having an Afternoon/Evening Out?

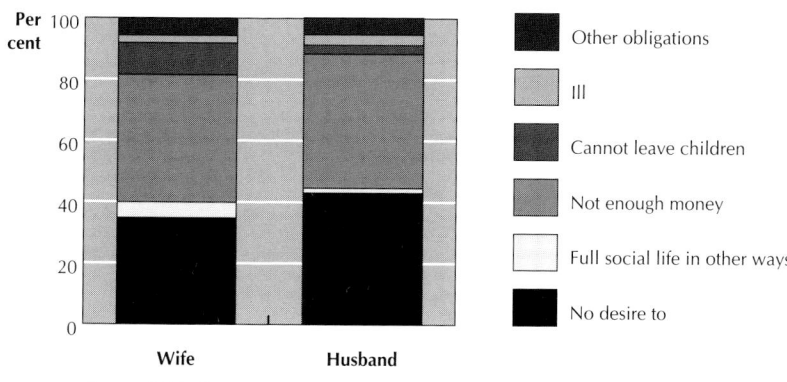

Source: Table D6

A lack of money is the most frequently given reason for staying at home, with *"no desire to do so"* accounting for a further 43 per cent of the husbands and 35 per cent of the wives. Those two reasons cover most of the respondents. However, children were cited by 10 per cent of the wives as the reason for not having time away from home the previous fortnight. In contrast, only 3 per cent of husbands cited children as the main reason for not going out. Overall, however, the dominant impression is one of similar experiences and similar reasons. Perhaps this is obvious. Married couples will tend to share similar preferences for using their leisure time, similar levels of sociability, and face the same basic financial constraints. In addition, presumably much of their socialising is done jointly. There remains scope, however, for inequality in how limited financial resources are spent, particularly when there is only one source of income. So, despite the substantial degree of consensus between husbands and wives that is portrayed, there is a sense in which some are more equal than others. This emerges if the focus is on those husbands and wives who indicate that they did not go out because of lack of money. When husbands give that response, 69 per cent of their wives give the same response, and 17 per cent of the wives indicate that *they* did have an afternoon or evening out. Where wives indicate that a lack of money prevented their having time away from home, 61 per cent of their husbands gave the same response to describe *their* own situation and 28 per cent report having gone out.

Thus far, the examination of household patterns has not looked systematically at the impact of income level, or the other socio-economic factors, on financial management, control, or household outcomes. Before concluding this descriptive chapter, it is useful to at least indicate the importance of such factors, which are the focus of the next chapter. Access to personal spending money at all levels of household income is consistently greater for husbands than for wives. Figure 4.5 groups households according to their disposable household income.

Figure 4.5 Percentage of Husbands and Wives with Personal Spending Money by Income Quintile

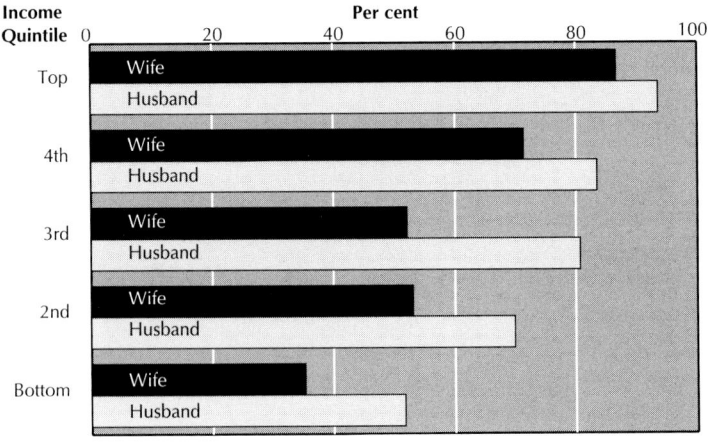

Source: Table D7

The gap between husbands and wives widens as we move down the income hierarchy. In the top quintile of households, 93 per cent of husbands and 87 per cent of wives have access to personal spending money. By the bottom quintile, only 52 per cent of the husbands and 35 per cent of wives report having money available to spend "*on yourself for your own pleasure or recreation*".

This is an appropriate point to conclude the description of how Irish families make financial decisions. A look at who has access to personal spending money reiterates the fundamental distinctions between management and control of household finances, between responsibility for spending and discretion over how it is spent. Further, consideration of personal spending money highlights the way in which income inequalities interact with gender inequalities, and do so in a manner that leaves wives in low income households doubly disadvantaged.

4.3 Conclusion

This chapter described the landscape of family financial decision-making in Ireland, in so far as can be revealed from the responses to the questions contained in the ESRI Panel Survey. At this point, some tentative conclusions can be made and some markers for further investigation can be identified.

The survey results provide evidence that "joint" decision-making is not necessarily a sign of equity. Overall, though, the levels of agreement between spouses are high. Spouses tend to agree in their description of the recent state of their household's finances. For making a big financial decision, couples overwhelmingly claimed that it would be a joint decision. Apparent consensus also prevails when asked to identify the most likely source of money to meet an emergency bill.

In relation to personal spending money, equity is greatest at the two extremes of the income distribution, that is, amongst the very poor and the very affluent households. However, in general, sharing within the family is less equitable. Husbands are consistently more likely to have access to money for their entertainment and to have more money to spend on their leisure whenever like households are compared with like. Thus, even where both husbands and wives work and both have access to personal spending money, husbands have the larger share.

CHAPTER FIVE

Explaining Variations in Financial Management Arrangements

5. Introduction

This chapter examines differences in family financial management and related features of family life and, where possible, offers an interpretation of patterns that emerge. In doing so, the analytical framework is the one developed in previous studies of income distribution and redistribution in Ireland (Rottman, Hannan *et al*, 1982: Rottman and Reidy, 1988). Social class and family cycle are the main dimensions by which households are differentiated. Social class represents fundamental differences in the nature and level of resources that families can use to earn an income. Differences among social classes can be understood as vertical inequalities among families, parallel to, but not identical in meaning to, income based differences. Stages of the family cycle correspond to horizontal inequalities among families in terms of need relative to "earning power" and indicate the ages of parents and children in a household.

Social classes and family cycle stages are augmented by measures that describe households in terms of disposable income, wife's labour force participation, farming vs. non-farming, and reliance on social welfare payments for income.[1] The underlying model of family dynamics assumes that background factors, such as income or social class, have an impact on both the type of financial management system being used by households and on outcomes, such as the equality with which spending money for personal leisure is distributed. That model informs the analysis reported in this chapter. Family cycle subsumes differences in the number of dependent children in a household relative to the number of potential income recipients. Given the number of factors and the ways in which they are measured, the chapter does not attempt to do more than establish the linkages between factors and to assess the broad plausibility of the model.

---

[1] (See Callan, Nolan *et al*, 1989 for a full discussion of how such factors are related to the risk of being in poverty)

Explaining Variations in Financial Management Arrangements

A summary of the factors under scrutiny is:

Background Factors	Financial Management System	Outcomes
Social Class	Income Sharing	Child Oriented
Income Level	Spheres of Expenditure Responsibility	Spousal Agreement
Wife Employment		Personal Leisure
Income Source		Personal Spending Money
Family Cycle Stage		Psychological Distress

The first step is to look at how management systems are distributed by such key household characteristics as social class, income level, and wife's labour force participation.

5.1 Variation in Management Systems

Higher incomes, multiple earners, and low levels of dependency in households all tend to make alternative financial management systems possible. Selecting the financial management system they would prefer is a luxury beyond the means of those households receiving a single low income and raising young children. Consequently, it should not be assumed that the degree to which various systems are present at particular income levels or in particular types of families is the result of the preferences or choices of household members.

Two aspects of financial management are at issue: one measures the degree of sharing and the other the existence of distinct expenditure spheres and responsibilities. Income level and source are the most basic ways for locating where households, using each sharing arrangement and each division of expenditure responsibility, are to be found. The five quintiles of households ranked by their disposable income provide a reasonable map of household financial well-being. Social class offers a somewhat different basis for distinguishing among families in terms of their resources and life styles. Social class in Ireland tends to reflect long-term factors, which change little across generations and hence indicate the relative advantage families enjoy in their life chances (see Whelan and Whelan, 1984; Breen *et al*, 1990). Farm households are traditionally viewed as operating distinctive internal systems of financial management. A high proportion of income from social welfare is expected to give additional force to the general tendency for whole wage/wife control to accompany low incomes.

Although the whole wage system (one person management) and joint management system[2] are the most common, the others represent potentially important ways for organising family finances in terms of the internal allocation of income and resources.

Differences in the type of financial management system being used according to social class, income level and income source, tend to conform to what studies in other countries report. Figure 5.1 looks at how expenditure responsibilities are divided in each income quintile. The bottom and the top quintiles provide a strong contrast. Wife managed households (equivalent to the whole wage system) are most common at the bottom of the income distribution. Wife management is used in 59 per cent of households in the bottom quintile, but only in 36 per cent of those in the top quintile. Husband management (ie the allowance system) is twice as common in the bottom as at the top quintile. Independent management is found in only 6 per cent of the bottom quintile households and 18 per cent of the top. The top and the bottom of the income distribution are, therefore, also distinctive in the degree to which independent management is practised in the former and wife management in the latter. The second lowest quintile also is more likely to use a whole wage system/wife management. There is little to differentiate among the top four quintiles in the prevalence of joint management.

Social class refers to differences in the economic and cultural resources that can be used to generate income and that are sufficiently strong to persist from one generation in a family to the next. As such, social classes represent categories of families that experience similar life chances, eg the likelihood of obtaining an adequate education, of finding secure employment, of remaining healthy. Social class is of particular importance in Ireland because, compared to other western democracies, the prospect of a child born into one class transferring into another through educational, occupational, or marriage mobility is low (Goldthorpe, 1987: Chapter 11; Erikson and

---

[2] For descriptions of the four main financial management systems used in this report see pages 9 and 40).

Goldthorpe, 1992; Breen, Whelan, and Whelan, 1992). A census-based definition of social class, through six categories, is used here, (see O'Hare *et al*, 1991 for background and specifications).[3]

Figure 5.1 Financial Management Systems: Differences by Income Quintiles

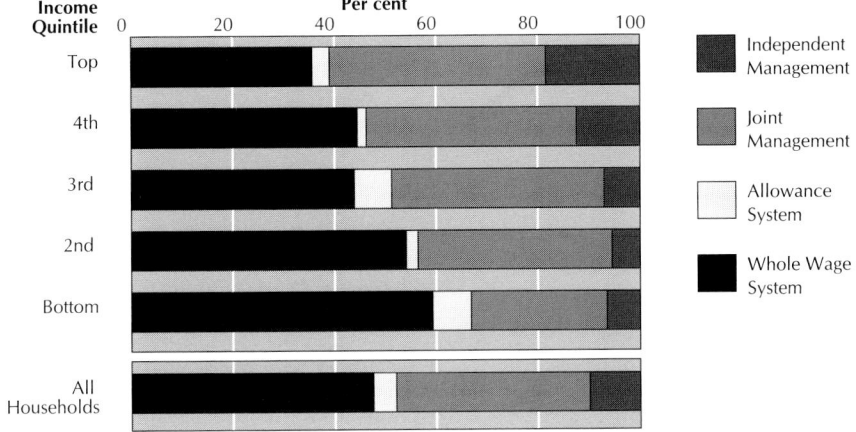

Key: Income quintiles group households on the basis of their total disposable incomes:

Bottom quintile:	Lowest	-	£127.94 per week
2nd quintile:	£127.95	-	£185.94 per week
3rd quintile:	£185.95	-	£247.27 per week
4th quintile:	£247.28	-	£329.42 per week
Top quintile:	£329.43	-	highest per week

Source: Table D8

The social classes and their respective choice of financial management system can be viewed in Figure 5.2. Social classes 1 and 2, with their concentration of professional and managerial households, tend to be distinctive. Both are particularly likely to use independent management, an arrangement that presupposes two incomes. The whole wage system/wife management accounts for less than one in five households in social class 1, compared to nearly one half in all other categories. Independent management is more common in social class 1 (20 per cent). Joint

---

[3] The distribution of heads of households and all persons by social class in the ESRI Phase 2 survey closely approximates that in the 1986 Census of Population, as shown in Appendix B. For a more detailed exposition of the meaning and importance of social class in the Irish context, see Breen et al, 1990: Chapters 3 and 4. The six classes are described in the key to Figure 5.2.

management is practised in 55 per cent of social class 1's households, compared to about one-third in the other social classes. Despite these differences, joint management is present, to roughly the same degree, in social classes 2 to 6, indicating the diversity of ways that households with similar income and other circumstances organise their finances.

Social class differences tend to persist when comparisons are restricted to households in which the wife either is or is not in employment. For example, households in social class 1 are substantially more likely than those in any of the other classes to use joint management even if only one spouse is in employment. In contrast, whole wage system/wife management is quite rare in social class 1 if the wife is employed, found in only 13 per cent of households compared to between 38 per cent and 78 per cent in the other class categories. Independent management becomes particularly pronounced amongst higher and lower professional households where both partners are working, describing 44 per cent and 47 per cent of households, respectively. The only other substantial presence of independent management is amongst skilled manual employees (social class 4), where it accounts for 26 per cent of the households where both partners are working. For the most part, both partners working does not greatly change the distribution of expenditure responsibility in the other social classes.[4]

Some effects related to income level appear to be enhanced or modified depending on the source of that income, as summarised in Figure 5.3. Farm income, for example, tends to promote whole wage system/wife management and diminishes the percentage of households using joint or independent management systems. Wife employment tends to promote independent management but not joint management. Where income is mainly from social welfare payments, whole wage system/wife management is prevalent, applying to 63 per cent of households. Allowance system/husband management occurs in 7 per cent of such households. Joint and independent management together thus account for less than one-third of households with, primarily, social welfare income.

---

[4] A note of caution: the number of households in each social class with a wife in employment is quite small, making percentages potentially misleading. The following numbers are involved by social class category: 1 (31 households); 2 (23); 3 (21); 4 (46); 5 (20); 6 (7).

Explaining Variations in Financial Management Arrangements

Figure 5.2 Financial Management Systems: Differences by Social Class

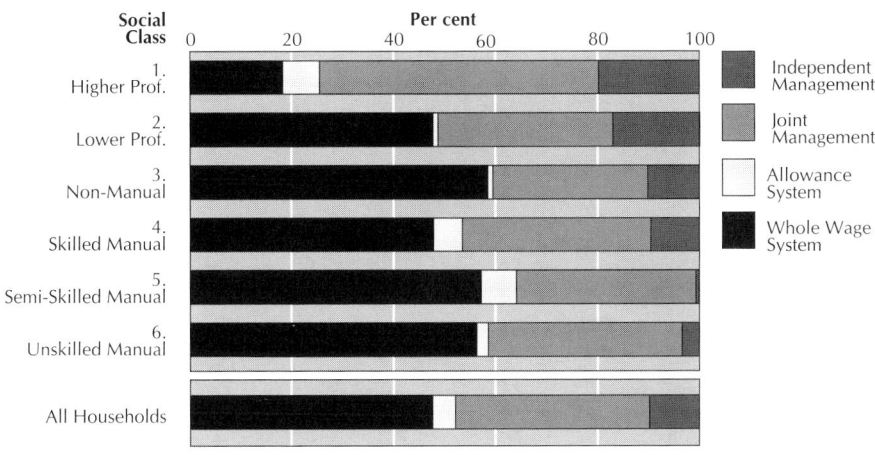

Key:

Social Class 1   Higher professional employees and self-employed; senior managers; larger proprietors; farmers with 200 or more acres.

Social Class 2   Lower professional employees; junior managers; small proprietors; farmers with 100-199 acres.

Social Class 3   Intermediate and other non-manual employees; farmers with 50-99 acres.

Social Class 4   Skilled manual employees and farmers with 30-49 acres.

Social Class 5   Semi-Skilled manual employees and farmers with less than 30 acres.

Social Class 6   Unskilled manual employees.

Source: Table D9

Figure 5.3 Financial Management Systems: Differences by Special Household Characteristics

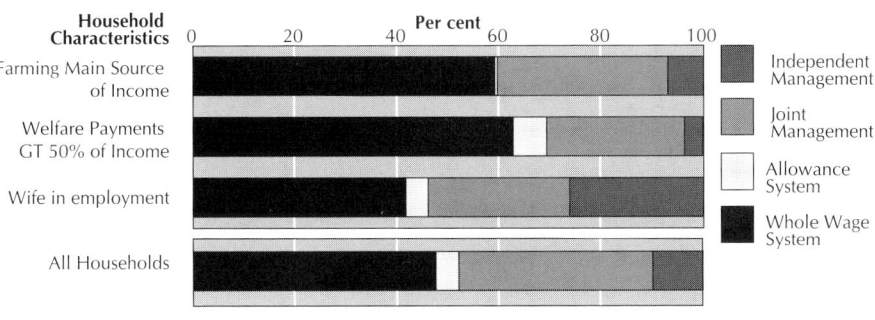

Source: Table D10

67

Finally, the presence of children, as well as stage in the family cycle affect the choice of management system within households. Figure 5.4 indicates the prevailing pattern. Childless households have a strong leaning towards the whole wage system/wife management, and independent management. Where children are present a number of distinctions are observed. In the child-rearing stage of the cycle (stage 3), the likelihood of independent management is reduced and the use of an allowance system/husband management slightly increased. Joint management is particularly common in the stages where young children are present, (stages 2 and 3). Whole wage system/wife management is especially prevalent in the early and late stages of the family cycle (stages 1 and 5); so too, however, is independent management. Family cycle stages thus differentiate among households in terms of the ages of children and spouses. It is of note, however, that the differences that are present across the family cycle do not provide evidence of generational change. Such change would be one possible interpretation if clear differences had emerged between households in early and late stages of the family cycle, since their occupants represent distinct generations. Instead, child-rearing responsibilities and labour market participation rates appear to be the most important considerations in the choice of management system. Overall, the similarities across the cycle outweigh the systematic differences present.

The extent of income sharing also differs according to basic household characteristics. Income level is the obvious point to start. Two indices will be examined. The first is the percentage of income that is shared (see Figure 5.5), either through allowances or contributions to a "kitty". This indexes how much of the income accruing to household members is made available for common consumption. The second characteristic refers to the degree to which such income as is being shared can be described as discretionary (see Figure 5.6). This is accomplished by expressing the weekly grocery bill as a percentage of a household's shared income.

Looking at Figure 5.5 it can be seen that there is a curvilinear relationship between the amount of household disposable income and the percentage of income that is shared, ie sharing is low in the top quintile (where 50 per cent of household income is made available for common use) and at the bottom (40 per cent is shared, on average). Sharing is most prevalent in the middle quintile, where, on average, household members share 70 per cent of their combined incomes.[5]

Explaining Variations in Financial Management Arrangements

Figure 5.4 Financial Management Systems: Differences by Family Cycle Stage

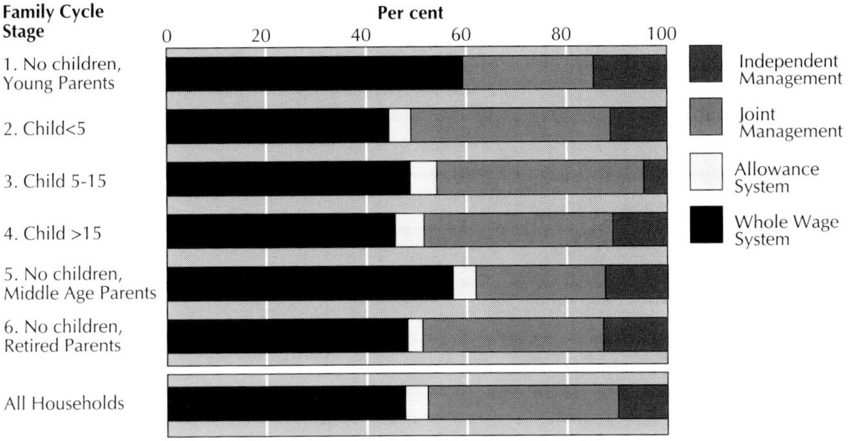

Key: Family Cycle Stage 1: Young married; no children in household.
      Family Cycle Stage 2: Child less than 5 years old present.
      Family Cycle Stage 3: Child between 5 and 15 years old present.
      Family Cycle Stage 4: Child older than 15 present.
      Family Cycle Stage 5: No children present; husband 40 to 65 years old and wife older than 45.
      Family Cycle Stage 6: No children present; husband aged 66 plus and wife older than 45.

Source: Table D11

The source of income is also important. Households with income derived mainly from social welfare payments typically share one-third of their income, compared to the average of almost two-thirds in other households.[6] The extent of sharing in households where the wife is in paid employment and in farm households is 59 per cent and 61 per cent respectively.

Social class and family cycle differences are evident but are not as substantial nor as clear as those found by income level and source. Sharing is most common in social class 3, which contains intermediate and other non-manual

---

[5] Standard deviations, shown in brackets in Table D12 (Appendix D), indicate how concentrated households in a particular income quintile, social class, or family cycle stage are around the average. Thus, the smaller the standard deviation the more concentrated observations are around the average.

[6] The mean for households receiving more than one-half of their income from social welfare has a standard deviation of 0.34, indicating very substantial variation within that category. In contrast, the standard deviation for other households is 0.30. The statistics refer to 146 and 440 households, respectively.

Figure 5.5 Income Sharing in Irish Households: Averages by Income Quintile, Social Class, Family Cycle, and Special Household Characteristics

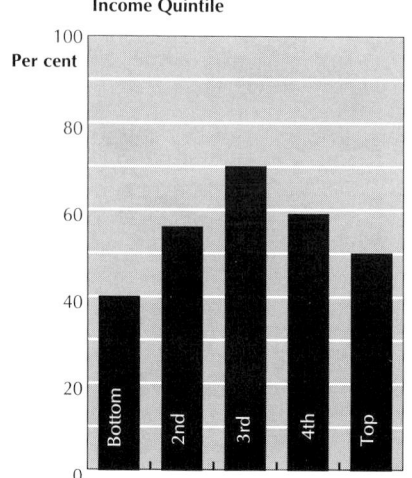

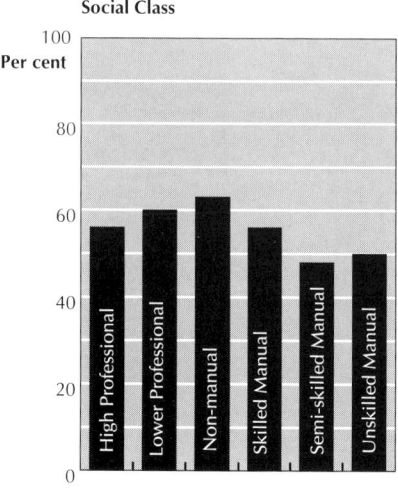

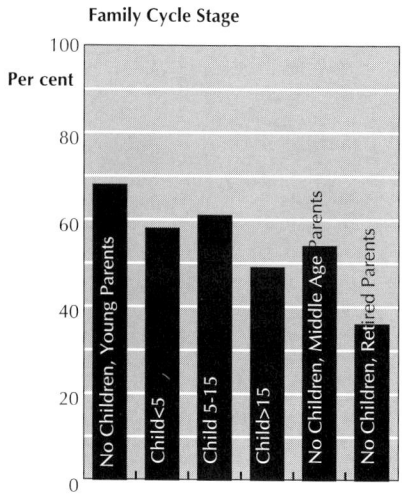

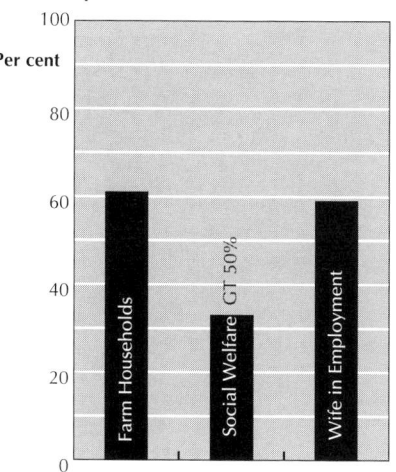

Source: Table D12

workers such as "service" workers and technicians, plus farmers owning 50-99 acres. Sharing appears to be most common at the initial stage of the family cycle, before children are born, and increases again in the stages in which children are present. The lowest level of sharing, on average, is in the late stage, when the care of young dependents has ceased.

The breath of expenditures covered by what is shared also varies according to income, social class, and family cycle. Figure 5.6 provides the details. Overall, expenditure on groceries accounts, on average, for 59 per cent of shared income. Most of what is shared in low income and working class households is spent on groceries and other daily essentials. This contrasts with the significant proportion of shared income available for other types of expenditure in households with high incomes, households at the start of the family cycle, and amongst the professional social classes. There is little discretionary shared income in farm households and in households dependent on social welfare payments as income. However, the percentage of shared income devoted to purchasing groceries is lower in households where both partners are in employment. As a result, while households at the top and the bottom of the income distribution tend to do the least income sharing, sharing at high income levels covers a range of expenditure, while the sharing at low income levels is used primarily to pay for day-to-day necessities.

5.2 Conclusion

In locating financial management systems on a sociological map of Irish society, two aspects of household allocation systems were stressed: how responsibilities for expenditure are divided between spouses and the percentage of income that is shared. These represent distinct but related dimensions of family financing. Social class, income level, and family cycle are the defining features of Irish society used here. Expenditure responsibilities tend to be concentrated in one person at high levels of sharing. Lower levels of sharing among household members open up possibilities for more elaborate divisions of responsibility for purchasing. Independent management is feasible only where both spouses have substantial income and can take direct responsibility for one or more expenditure spheres. The divisions appear, however, to typically follow traditional gender-based distinctions in which the wife as household manager takes primary responsibility for day to day essentials and the husband for large recurrent expenses, such as rent.

Figure 5.6 Groceries as a Percentage of Shared Income: Averages by Income Quintile, Social Class, Family Cycle and Special Household Characteristics

Income Quintile

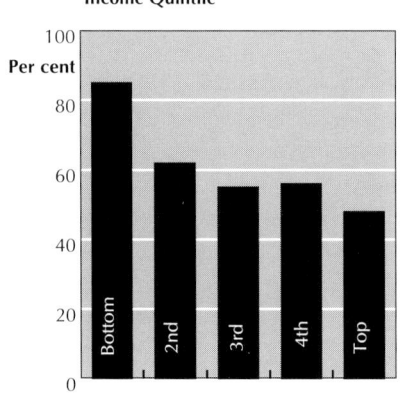

Social Class

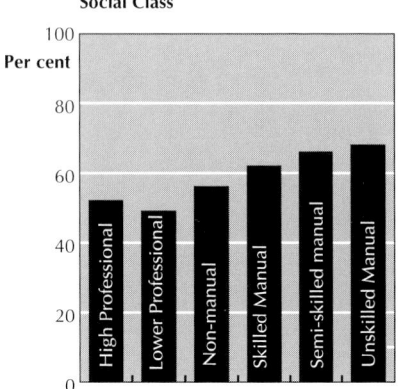

Family Cycle Stage

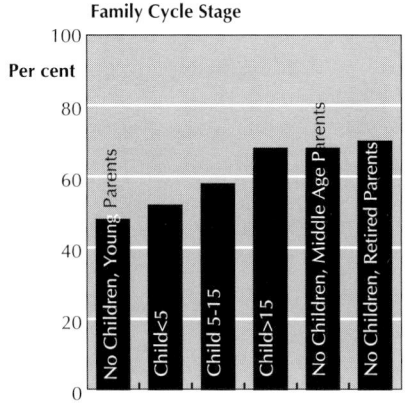

Special Household Characteristic

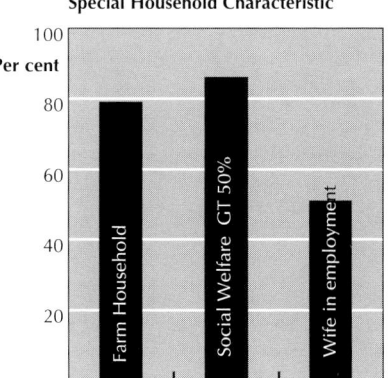

Source: Table D13

Explaining Variations in Financial Management Arrangements

Sharing of income tends to be greatest in households located in the middle of the income distribution. Households in the bottom and top of the income distribution tend to be considerably less likely than those in the middle to share a major proportion of their earnings. This may, in part, reflect a concentration of dual earner households at middle range incomes and of single income households following the traditional working class practice of whole wage management. Families that receive most of their income in the form of social welfare payments tend to share low amounts of their incomes. The interpretation and consideration of the implications of that low average is complicated by the substantial diversity in sharing arrangements found among those households.

CHAPTER SIX

Financial Management and the Well-Being of Households and Persons

6. Introduction

Do differences in income sharing and in how expenditure responsibilities are divided matter for the well-being of households and individual household members? This chapter looks at a number of key indicators of the outcomes experienced collectively and individually by spouses in the 625 families which participated in the 1989 survey.

The term "household outcomes" refers to the diverse ways in which resources other than income are shared within households. This ranges from the degree of agreement on financial matters, the access to personal spending money and the amount available for that purpose, to the priority given to different spending areas. Consideration is also given to indices of psychological health. The division of expenditure responsibility, as defined in the preceding chapters, is used to investigate the effect of financial management on such outcomes.

Does the degree to which income received, and responsibilities for expenditure, are shared within households affect the internal allocation of resources? A straightforward answer is not possible. It is possible, however, to find statistically significant relationships between sharing and, say, wives' access to personal spending money. But, as we have just seen, households share in ways that are related to their incomes, social class, family cycle stage, and other characteristics. To authoritatively disentangle the factors underlying differences among households, in what we have termed outcomes, so as to distinguish the role of income *per se* from how that money is allocated requires complex multivariate statistical analysis. The approach taken in this report is to focus on those relationships between sharing and outcomes that seem to stand independently even when income level has been taken into consideration.

6.1 Agreement on Financial Matters

Do spouses agree on financial matters? We have found that yes, by and large, spouses agree. Spouses in more than two out of three households agree on all of the five questions relating to family finances considered in this chapter.[1]

Figure 6.1 looks at the number of disagreements found in households according to the financial management system used. There is marked similarity in the number of disagreements across the range of financial management systems, with some minor variations on the main theme. While two-thirds of spouses are in agreement on financial matters across management systems, disagreements appear slightly more common in households using independent management for expenditures, eg there are disagreements in 36 per cent of the independent management households, compared to between 31 per cent in the allowance system and 35 per cent of those using the whole wage system; (joint management 33 per cent). This difference, though slight relative to the overwhelming levels of agreement reported, suggests that there is more scope for differences of opinion in independently managed households.

Figure 6.1 Disagreement Between Spouses on Financial Matters

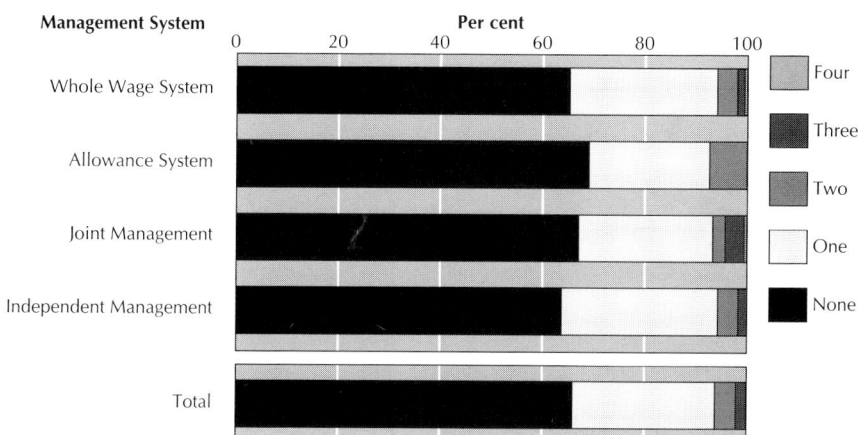

Source: Table D14

Whether spouses agree in how they would make a financial decision in an emergency situation also varies depending on their choice of allocation system.

---

[1] The five questions were: (1) "Has your overall financial situation... (5 choices)?"; (2) "Within the last 12 months, has it ever happened that you were unable to pay your mortgage, rent, gas, or ESB?"; (3) "Within the past 12 months, has it ever happened that you had to go into debt to pay your mortgage, rent, gas, or ESB?"; (4) "Within the past 12 months, has it ever happened that you had to go into debt to pay other ordinary living expenses?"; and (5) "Within the past 12 months, have you had to do without things you feel are really essential for you or your family in order to pay the mortgage, rent, gas, or ESB...(5 choices)?" Five options were offered for the first and last question; the other three questions were phrased to elicit a yes/no response. The results were presented in Table 4.1.

Both spouses were asked who would decide on how to meet an unforeseen emergency expense: the husband, the wife, or jointly. Figure 6.2 compares the responses given by husbands and wives according to financial management system used. Joint decision-making is the predominant and agreed choice in all but those households that adopt an allowance system of management.

Although there are only 17 (reweighted) households in this category for examination in Figure 6.2, the responses are in accord with what research in other countries suggests; that is, that the extent of control that such a system entails for the main earner, usually the husband, is in dispute in nearly one-half of the households. It is worth noting that joint and independent provision for expenditure does not preclude responses suggestive of husband control of household finances.[2]

Figure 6.2 Who Would Decide on How to Resolve a Financial Emergency: Husband and Wife Responses by Financial Management System

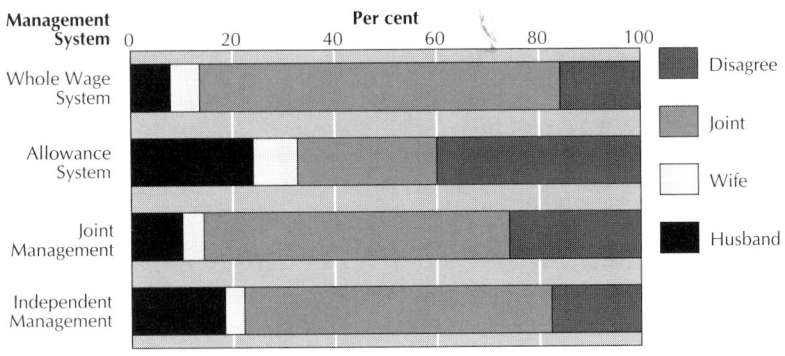

Source: Table D15

Husband control, as indexed by agreement that the husband would decide how to meet an emergency expense, is promoted where either very little or most of the household's income is shared. Joint decisions are cited less frequently by the spouses in such households, but the difference is slight. Income sharing, this suggests, cannot be equated with joint control over household finances.

---

[2]   The co-existence of "independent" management and husband "control" is also present in British studies (Pahl, 1989:82; Vogler, 1989).

On balance, the contents of Figure 6.2 support the contention by Pahl and others that "management" and "control" are distinct aspects of family financial management (see Chapter 1 of this report for a summary of their reasoning). Sharing of money and expenditure responsibilities (as expressed through the different choices of financial management systems), do not inexorably erode gender inequalities in the distribution of power within marriages. However, this study, like most previous forays into the topic of family finances, is heavily weighted toward material describing management systems; only one question (on emergency expenses) even indirectly serves as an indicator for control.[3]

6.2 Access to Personal Money and to Leisure

Does the type of financial management system in place have implications for the distribution of personal spending money and opportunities for personal leisure within households? A simple index of the degree of inequality that is present between the spouses is to compare instances where either one or both has access to personal spending money. Equity in that regard is greatest in households with independent management systems, and least where an allowance system operates ie where the main earner controls expenditure, see Figure 6.3.

Figure 6.3 Access to Personal Spending Money: Husband and Wife Responses by Financial Management System

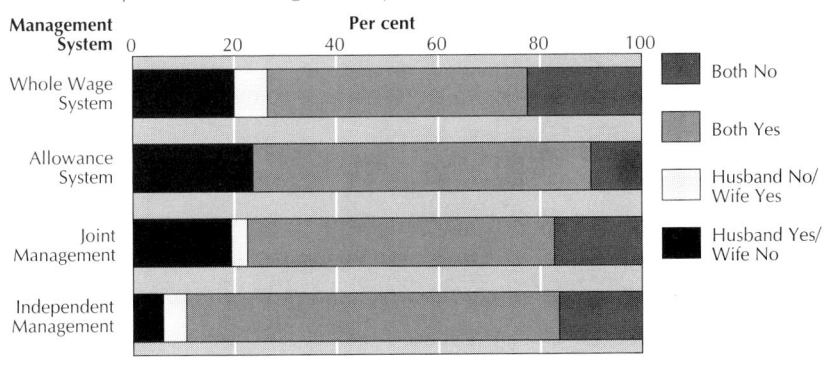

Source: Table D16

---

[3] Pahl's (1991) recent work stresses the degree to which ideologies about family life vivify the allocation systems based on who manages into gradations of domestic power and control. See the work of Vogler (1989) for a survey-based inquiry into attitudes relating to family financial management.

In Figure 6.3 responses by the husband and wife in each household are combined into four possible answers. Where independent management prevails, in only 6 per cent of households the husbands have personal spending money but their wives do not; in 5 per cent this is reversed. In nearly three-quarters both have personal spending money, and in a further 16 per cent neither spouse has access to money for their own use. By contrast, in all other types of financial management systems, differences between spouses tend to favour the husband, with the husband being the sole possessor of personal spending money in about one-fifth of all households. In general, it is important to note that in most households husbands and wives are equally situated: either both have personal spending money or neither does.

The amount of money available for personal spending also varies depending on the prevailing management system. In fact, the choice of financial management system is a better predictor than the level of household income in assessing how much personal spending money is available to husbands and wives, with a considerably more substantial predictive relationship for wives than for husbands.[4]

This relationship is presented in terms of averages in Figure 6.4 which show that wives have more money available for personal spending in independently managed households (£22); and least money available in households using an allowance system (£6).

Households using whole wage/wife management systems and joint management households are similar and fall somewhere between the other two, with £11 and £12 respectively, on average, available as wives' personal expenditure money. In practice, this is due to low levels of personal spending money in households using an allowance system, and high levels of personal spending money in independently managed households.

---

[4]   That assessment is based on multiple regression equations that predict the amount of money available for those husbands and those wives who report having money for their own use. The issue is whether the type of financial management system can explain variation in the amount of personal spending money and can do so independent of the effect associated with the amount of income flowing into a household.

The impact of the adopted financial management system is also evident in relation to access to leisure and recreation. Indeed, the differences are somewhat clearer than those found for access to speding money. In Figure 6.5, the situation of the, admittedly small (27), number of households using an allowance system sets a benchmark for comparing the other categories. In one-third of such households, the husband, but not the wife, reported having had "*an afternoon or evening out in the last fortnight*", compared to 63 per cent of households in the category where both spouses either had or had not had such leisure time. In the other categories, the inequity between husbands and wives is less pronounced. Approximately 15 per cent of the husbands, but not the wives, had an afternoon or evening out; in a smaller percentage of households that was reversed, with wives, but not husbands, having an afternoon or evening out (3 to 11 per cent). Where management is independent, 82 per cent of couples gave the same response. This compares to 75 per cent in households practising whole wage management and a virtually identical 74 per cent in jointly managed households.

Figure 6.4 Wives' Personal Expenditure Money by Financial Management System

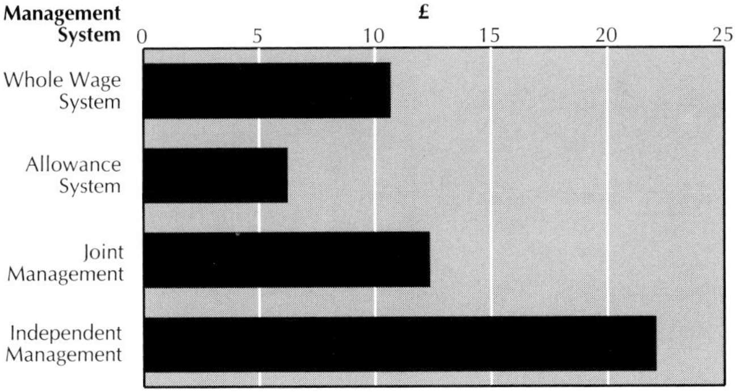

Source: Table D17

Figure 6.5 Did You Have an Afternoon or Evening Out in Last Fortnight?
Differences by Financial Management System

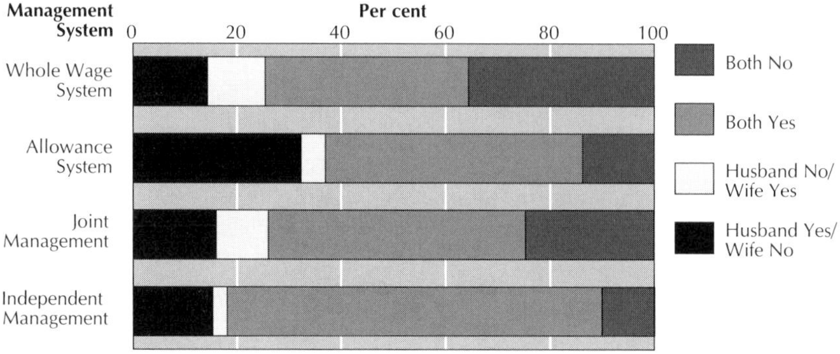

Source: Table D18

Overall, it can be concluded that financial management arrangements do affect the way in which husbands and wives experience outcomes such as access to personal spending money and opportunities for leisure and recreation. While the effects are rarely dramatic, there is some difference in the standard of living husbands and wives experience, depending on the financial management system adopted within the household. Because this study is the first of its kind in this country, and one of the few anywhere, to tackle these issues using a large-scale survey, the classifications being used are relatively crude. That differences nevertheless emerge with a reasonable degree of clarity is evidence for tying levels of well-being enjoyed by households members to the nature of the financial management system being used, at least in a general way.

6.3 Psychological Distress

Are the consequences of financial management systems limited to material standards of living or do they have psychological effects on the persons involved? The question is really whether sharing of income and expenditure responsibilities has an impact independent from that of other factors known to affect levels of psychological distress and a sense of fatalism. The answer is a cautious yes. Statistically significant relationships link income sharing to levels of psychological distress and feelings of fatalism and loss of control. Sharing of income is associated with lower levels of psychological distress and lower levels of fatalism. What is important, however, is not so much the percentage of income that is shared but the absolute amount of money that is available for common consumption. In all of these relationships, the effects are stronger for wives than for husbands. There is also an identifiable link between the way expenditure responsibilities are divided and the level of psychological distress, although here the relationship is similar for husbands and wives.[5]

The main findings from the analysis conducted in this study are as follows. The amount of shared income has a statistically significant *negative* effect on the level of psychological distress experienced by wives but not by husbands. The result is a very modest increment to the amount of variation that can be explained by reference to a household's social class and reliance on welfare income; in other words, the larger the amount that is shared, the lower the level of psychological distress. However, the type of financial management system in place explains, for both husbands and wives, a small, but statistically significant, additional percentage of the variation in psychological distress. A similar, but more deeply etched pattern emerges for the equations predicting levels of fatalism. For wives, but not for husbands, the amount of shared income has a negative effect on feelings of fatalism or powerlessness. For both spouses, the type of financial management system being used predicts the presence of a sense of fatalism or powerlessness.

Total household income and the amount of shared income were also used as predictors of fatalism and powerlessness. Again, the results clearly signal that it is how much is shared, rather than the amount of income accruing to household members, that predicts levels of psychological distress and

---

[5]   Multiple regression is used to establish the degree to which allocation-related variables can predict psychological health. Psychological distress is measured by the widely used 12 item General Health Questionnaire (GHQ) scale. Full details on the construction and validation of the scale are available in Whelan *et al*, 1991, Chapter 3, and the results of extensive analysis of explanatory factors using Irish data (Phase 1 of the ESRI panel study) can be found in Chapter 7 of that study. Fatalism is measured on a seven-item scale on which low scores indicate a feeling of "mastery" and high scores of fatalism or powerlessness (see Whelan *et al*, 1991:111-113). The measure of how well the predictors succeed is the R-squared, which indicates the percentage of all the variation in the criterion that is being explained, net of what is explained by basic socio-economic factors. To simplify the presentation of the results, two such factors are used: social class and reliance on social welfare. For further details see Appendix C.

fatalism.[6] It is reasonable to conclude that the absolute amount of income that is shared is a better predictor of psychological distress and of fatalism than is the total amount of income flowing into the household, and that this holds for both husbands and wives. Of course, income and the amount being shared are highly correlated.

Given the nature of the links identified and the qualifications noted in Appendix C, the main implication is to reinforce the importance of paying attention to how families organise their finances. How income and expenditure responsibilities are shared affects the material and psychological well-being of family members, but the effects are particularly evident for wives.

6.4 Conclusion

Overall, the sharing of responsibilities, expressed in the way financial decision making is organised, appears to be more consequential for what occurs within families than the degree of income sharing itself. The level of disagreement on financial matters, spending priorities, and the equity with which personal leisure and personal spending money are distributed are most strongly associated with how expenditure responsibilities are divided. The nature of that association also is reasonably amenable to interpretation.

The psychological consequences of financial management for wives appear to be more directly linked to the degree to which income is shared. There is also evidence to suggest that how responsibilities are divided leads to higher or lower levels of psychological distress or feelings of fatalism for both spouses. The connection between sharing and psychological health is

---

[6] Total income was entered first, and then total income and shared income in a subsequent equation, resulting in total income becoming insignificant and shared income, generally, having a statistically significant effect. The amounts of total income and of shared income are of course related: they have a correlation of 0.61. To ensure that collinearity was not distorting the results, the predictive equations were also run using a measure of shared income that has relationships to psychological distress and feelings of fatalism that are net of whatever impact can be attributed to the size of total household income. This entails (a) finding the predicted value of shared income by regressing that variable on total household disposable income and (b) subtracting the predicted amount of shared income from the actual amount shared and using the result as a new variable. Stated briefly, the "residual" shared income variable has a correlation of zero with total household disposable income. The basic findings are replicated when the residual measure is used in the regressions.

complex. At the core, however, what matters is the absolute amount of income that is shared. Substantial sums may be earned by household members, but where it is not made available for common use, psychological distress and feelings of fatalism are likely to be higher than would otherwise be the case. Similarly, the level of income may be moderate, but where it is shared the degree of psychological distress and feelings of fatalism experienced by spouses will be reduced relative to other households where sharing is less extensive. These effects can be identified for both husbands and wives, but generally the link to women's psychological well-being is stronger.

CHAPTER SEVEN

Earnings, Child Benefit and the Economic Status of Women

7. Introduction

Women in nearly one-half of the families in the survey reported having an independent source of earned income, while 70 per cent of the families received Child Benefit payment, which is money that is paid directly to the wife. This chapter looks at the impact that such income has on financial management arrangements and on spending patterns in households. The main questions considered are: How important are women's earnings and Child Benefit payments for the overall economic well-being of the household and of individual household members? To what extent, and in what ways, are women's earnings and Child Benefit different from other income sources?

7.1 Women's Incomes

Overall, wives' earnings account for 14 per cent of the total disposable (post-tax) income received by the 625 families (see Table 3.1, Chapter 3). Where the wife has an income, it constitutes 26 per cent of total income; where the wife is in employment, her contribution represents 35 per cent of all income received.

One way to gauge the importance of Child Benefit payments is to estimate the number of families with dependent children in which payments are the largest source of income received directly by the mother. There are 414 households in the sample that receive Child Benefit. Among those households 58 per cent of wives have no other source of income; for 10 per cent of wives there is income from employment or interest, that on a weekly basis is less than what Child Benefit provides; and wives' earnings in 32 per cent of households exceed the amount that is derived through Child Benefit. Women who work are slightly more likely than those who do not work to have income from a bank account or other investments.[1] But a second source of income is rare: women in only one in twelve families with dependent children (8 per cent), and one in ten (10 per cent), of all families had an income that was drawn from more than one of the following sources: employment, self-employment, social welfare, interest or rent and occupational pensions.

On a straightforward accountancy basis, Child Benefit is therefore the largest source of independent income available to women in two out of every three families with dependent children. Figure 7.1 allows us to make some finer distinctions among households, specifically in relation to their social class and

---

[1]   Interest income accrues directly to 19 per cent of women not at work, compared to 31 per cent of those who are employed or self-employed.

level of disposable income, in order to establish the degree of variation in direct access to earnings by women. A profile of wives' earnings is offered for each social class category, and each income quintile, in terms of the percentage with (a) no independent earnings; (b) earnings that amount to less than the Child Benefit payments received; and (c) where earnings are greater than Child Benefit. Earnings in excess of the money that women receive through Child Benefit are typical in none of the categories. However, social class and income levels are both strongly related to the percentage of households in which the woman has either a small independent income (small relative to what Child Benefit provides) or earns a sum greater than what Child Benefit makes available.[2] Among families in the unskilled manual category, 80 per cent of women have no independent income other than Child Benefit; in about eight out of every ten households in the bottom three income quintiles women have no independent income or that income falls below what Child Benefit provides. Interest earned from a separate savings account is the standard independent source of a wives' income that provides less money than does Child Benefit.

Figure 7.1 Households with Dependent Children: Wives' Income Status by Social Class and Total Household Income

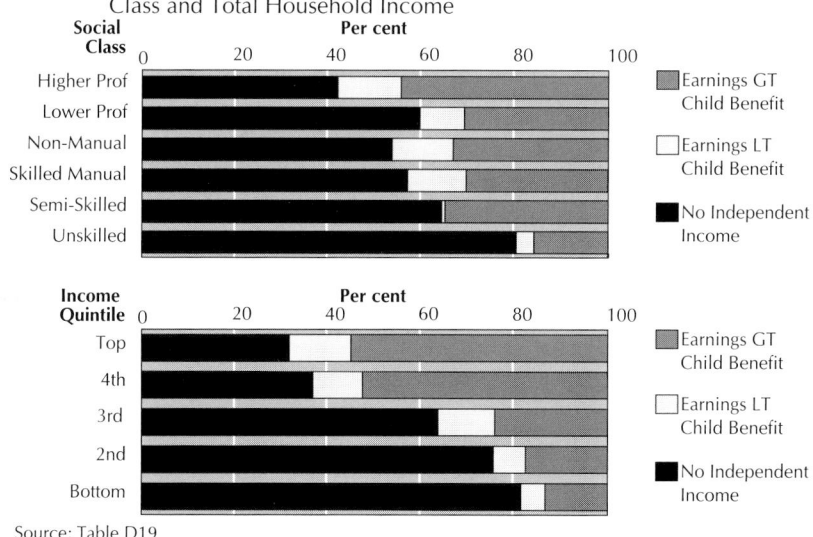

Source: Table D19

---

[2] Of course, dual-earner households typically, but not inevitably, will rank in the upper income quintiles. The quintile ranking, however, includes households in which the wife is the sole or main earner (see Figure 3.2, Chapter 3) for an indication of the prevalence of such households.

7.2 The Uses of Women's Earnings

If the female partner had a source of income from outside the household, she was asked to estimate how it was divided for six specific purposes which are listed in Figure 7.2, along with the average percentage given for each purpose. A seventh "miscellaneous" category was used to cater for responses that fell outside of the six possibilities provided by the interviewer.

Figure 7.2 How Women's Income is Usually Spent

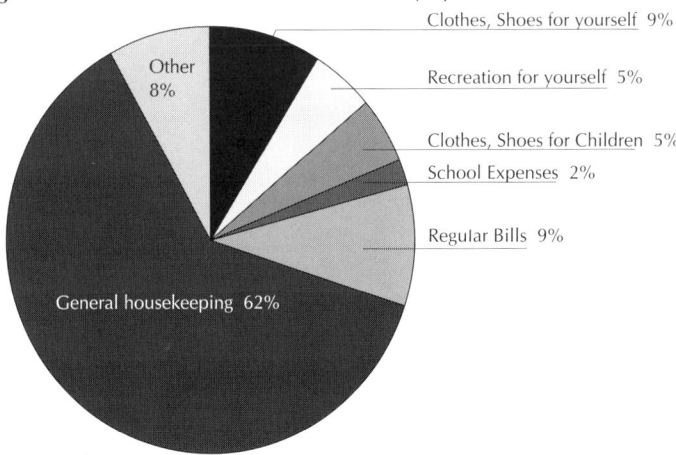

Source: Table D20

There is a strong pattern of women's incomes being devoted to family rather than personal expenditures, and an equally strong tendency for the contribution to go to general purposes. It remains possible, of course, that this is obscuring differences between families in which there are dependent children (defined here as less than age 16) and those in which there are either no children or children in their late teens or older. To investigate that possibility, the spending areas are divided into three: (a) spending on one's own clothing or entertainment; (b) spending on children; and (c) general household expenses. The relative share of women's income that each area receives can be seen in Figure 7.3, which compares households with children to those without children.

The presence of school age children does have an impact on the self-reported uses made of women's incomes, with an apparent shift from personal spending to spending on the children. The importance of dependent children for wives' incomes is most evident in the contrast between the 31 per cent of women with children who report no personal expenditure from their incomes and the 12 per cent of women without dependent children who report a similar lack of personal benefit. However, divergence between the two groups of women is quite modest, overshadowed by the general trend for women's income to be directed at the household's general needs. Just over half of each group spends more than three-quarters of their income on the household; seven out of ten women in both groups report that more than half of their income goes to general household expenses. The converse is that it is rare for women's earnings to be spent on their personal consumptions; only 18 per cent of women with dependent children spend more than one quarter of their incomes on personal items, as do 10 per cent of those without dependent children.[3]

Figure 7.3 Distribution of Women's Income by Purpose: Families With and Without Dependent Children

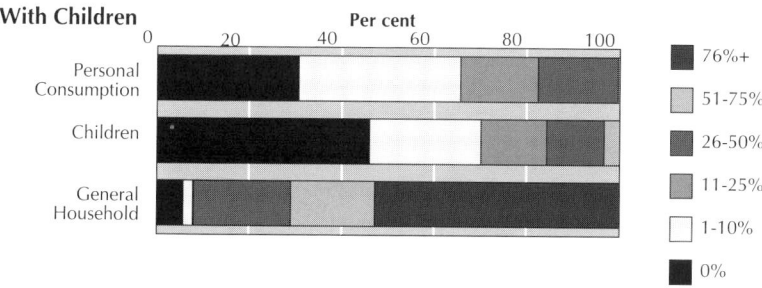

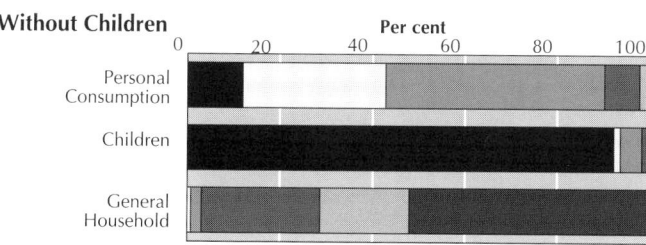

Source: Table D21

Note : Each bar refers to one of the three spending areas and indicates the distribution of women according to the proportion of their incomes allocated to specific spending areas.

---

[3] We unfortunately lack comparable data on husbands' spending, which could exhibit quite similar patterns to that found for wives.

On balance, women's earnings tend to supplement the general household finances, rather than being used for their personal expenditure or being directed at meeting the specific costs of child rearing. This may be a reflection of the pressing financial needs of the households in which women seek employment. However, while this may accurately describe the situation in a minority of households with both partner's working, the tendency is for dual income families to be in the upper part of the income distribution. There is also no evidence that the use of women's income varies depending on either the amount of income available to the household in total or the amount of money earned by the wife.[4]

Moreover there is no evident relationship between the amount that women earn and how that money is spent, although the relative contribution made by the two spouses does have an independent effect on the degree to which women's earnings are added to general housekeeping expenses. Generally, but particularly in families without dependent children, the relative sizes of husbands' and wives' earnings affect how much of women's incomes goes to regular household expenses. The more equal the spouses' incomes, the lower the share of the wives income being contributed to general household expenditure.[5]

7.3 Child Benefit
The control and use of Child Benefit payments is of particular interest

---

[4] Total household income has a modest, but statistically significant (-0.19, significant at the 0.05 level), negative correlation with the proportion of the women's income being used for general household expenses. That relationship is stronger (-0.31, significant at the 0.05 level) for households without children but is not present for households with dependent children.

[5] These relationships are confirmed when multiple regression techniques are used to test for whether these effects are independent (say, household income from equality of income contributions) and when the relationship between income and its use is expressed as curvilinear. The "R-squared" statistic indicating the proportion of variation explained is modest, as are the individual variable effects, but equality of income contribution appears to be more important than the income size of either the wife or of the household. Perhaps the most important feature of correlation and regression analysis, however, is the absence of a clear relationship between income size and whether it is used for personal expenditures, child-related expenses, or as part of the general household budget. There is simply little variation in the uses to which women report putting their incomes: at all income levels, and whether there are dependent children or not, women's incomes are apparently shared with the household.

because it is the one source of state income support that is paid directly to the mother. Where a household was receiving Child Benefit, the household manager was asked who decides how it is spent: (a) "usually the wife"; (b) "usually the husband"; or (c) "usually a joint decision". The responses from the 367 households receiving Child Benefit (the question was not answered in four of the applicable households) are shown in Figure 7.4. In most households, women control the use of Child Benefit. This leads to two further issues. Firstly, how Child Benefit is used. Secondly, does that use depend on whether the decision is made by the wife or jointly.

Figure 7.4 Who Decides How to Spend the Child Benefit?

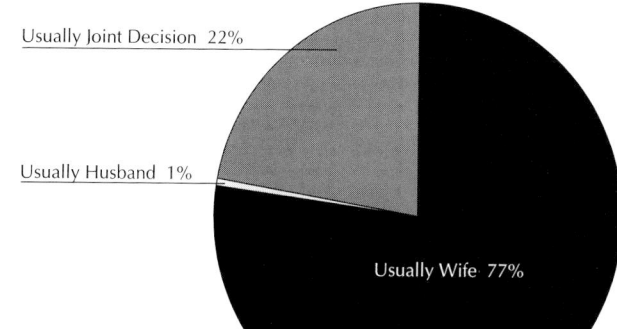

Usually Joint Decision 22%

Usually Husband 1%

Usually Wife 77%

Source: Table D22

Households tend to divide fairly evenly into those that usually spend their Child Benefit on general costs of living and those spending it on child specific purchases (most of the "other" uses supplied by respondents fall into the latter category). That balance seems, however, to differ between households where the decision on spending the money is jointly made and where it is taken by the wife. Figure 7.5 presents the relevant comparisons. Where the wife makes the decision, 46 per cent of the households claim that the money goes for general housekeeping and regular bills and 44 per cent for child specific expenses. The corresponding breakdown for "joint decision" households is 74 per cent and 18 per cent, respectively. That difference is statistically significant and suggests that a distinction might usefully be drawn in subsequent analyses between two types of child-rearing households: those in which Child Benefit is spent through a joint decision and those in which it is spent directly by the wife.

Figure 7.5 Use of Child Benefit by Decision Maker

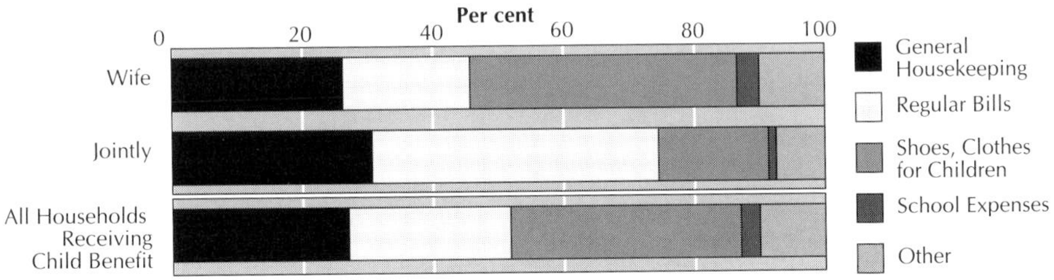

Source: Table D23

The potential importance of that distinction is supported by systematic differences in the composition of "joint" and "wife" control over Child Benefit. Households reporting joint control over how Child Benefit is spent tend to be those in which women have an independent source of income.[6] This means that the more equal the contributions made by the husband and wife, the more likely that they decide jointly on how to spend Child Benefit. It appears that it is the relative contributions made by the spouses that is important. The higher the husband's income, the *less* likely it becomes for the use of Child Benefit to be decided jointly.[7] There is a complex underlying inter-relationship between the husband's earnings, whether the wife works, and the equality of contributions to the total household income.[8] Further analysis suggests that the equality of spouses'

---

[6] For example, the correlation between who controls Child Benefit and an index of equality of the spouses' contributions to household income is 0.20 (significant at the 0.01 level, two-tailed test).

[7] The correlation here is negative -0.15, which is statistically significant at the 0.01 level.

[8] Probit analysis was used, which is a statistical technique for determining the independent and combined effects of predictor variables on a dependent variable.

contributions has an independent effect on who spends the Child Benefit payments, making it more likely that the decision will be a joint one. The size of the husband's income also has an independent effect. There is, however, no perceptible effect from the ages or number of children in the household.

It is worth noting here, however, that women's access to personal spending money sheds some additional light on what is revealed by knowing who decides on the use of Child Benefit. In contrast to other forms of income, it was found that shared or joint use of Child Benefit places women at a financial disadvantage. This extends to personal spending money: 44 per cent of women in households making joint decisions on Child Benefit have access to personal spending money, compared to 56 per cent in households where women spend the Child Benefit. Further, in households where Child Benefit is spent jointly, husband/wife differences in the amount of personal spending money are particularly wide.[9]

7.4 Spending Priorities

This leads to consideration of the more general topic of household spending priorities. The priorities selected by husbands and wives from the same list can be seen in Table 7.1. They were responding to the question of what would be the first priority in spending an increase of, say, £20 per week on household income. With eight possible responses, husbands and wives agree in 43 per cent of the households. Women, however, are substantially more likely to cite children's clothing as the first priority: 18 per cent of wives made that choice, compared to 10 per cent of husbands. The reverse is true for the choice of savings, selected by 13 per cent of husbands and 8 per cent of wives. Overall, the similarities in the patterns of response tend to overwhelm the points of departure in what is given emphasis.

---

[9] The differences in wives' access and in the amount of personal spending money are statistically significant using standard analysis of variance tests. A statistically significant difference to the amounts available is also found when the comparison is restricted to households in which the wives have personal spending money.

Table 7.1 First Spending Priority of an Increase of, say, £20 per week in Total Household Income*

Husband's Response:	Wife's Response								
	More/ Better Food	Childrens Clothes/ Shoes	Adults Clothes	Regular Bills	School Expenses	Clear Debts	Save	Home Repairs	Total
	Per Cent of All Households								
More/Better Food	11.7	1.9	1.7	2.1	0.0	0.9	0.9	0.7	**20.1**
Childrens Clothes/Shoes	1.1	5.6	0.9	0.8	0.1	0.5	0.3	0.4	**9.5**
Adults Clothes/Shoes	0.9	0.7	2.3	0.4	0.0	0.1	0.4	0.5	**5.2**
Regular Bills	3.1	4.2	0.8	7.9	0.4	1.1	0.8	0.0	**18.6**
School Expenses	1.3	1.1	0.2	0.0	0.7	0.1	0.1	0.1	**4.0**
Clear Debts	0.7	0.6	0.3	2.7	0.2	6.9	0.8	0.8	**13.0**
Save	2.1	1.6	1.3	0.9	0.2	0.8	4.0	1.0	**13.3**
Home Repairs	0.6	1.0	0.0	0.8	0.1	0.6	0.5	4.0	**8.1**
Total	**21.6**	**17.8**	**9.0**	**15.7**	**1.7**	**11.5**	**8.4**	**9.5**	**100.0** (N=610)

* Row totals refer to responses by husbands and column totals to the responses by wives for each option (eg 20.1% of husbands and 21.6% of wives chose "more/better food" as their first priority). The row and column totals do not add to 100 per cent because some categories are omitted: eg holidays (the choice of 2.2 per cent of wives and 2.5 per cent of husbands) and a miscellaneous "other" category (accounting for 2.5 per cent of wives' choices and 5.5 per cent of husbands' choices).

For families with children, whether there is "joint" or "wife" control of Child Benefit offers a promising basis for distinguishing households. That distinction rests on the responses given to two questions by a single member of the household. Nonetheless, there is evidence from other questions asked of both spouses about spending priorities that tends to reinforce confidence in the distinction's importance. Three general orientations in priorities are of particular interest: child-specific spending, essentials (food and reducing debt), and regular bills. Table 7.2 summarises the responses made by husbands and wives, differentiating between households in which Child Benefit is described as being spent by the wife or being spent jointly.

Table 7.2 First Spending Priorities: By Gender and Child Benefit Decision

First Priority	Who Decides on Child Benefit?	
	Wife	Jointly
	Per Cent	
Child		
Husband	22.4	14.8
Wife	30.0	23.4
Essentials		
Husband	33.9	33.9
Wife	32.7	41.4
Regular Bills		
Husband	15.3	21.0
Wife	16.0	20.9
	(N=281)	(N=81)

Although husbands and wives, in general, differ in the priority placed on the three spending areas, the responses also correspond to the different orientations found for the use of Child Benefit. In households where the wife decides how to spend Child Benefit payments, 22 per cent of husbands and 30 per cent of wives chose a child-specific item as their first priority for an increase to the household's regular income. That was the first priority for 15 per cent of the husbands and 23 per cent of the wives in households where the decision on how to spend Child Benefit is made jointly. There is also some evidence that there is greater agreement on spending priorities in households reporting that Child Benefit is spent jointly. Spouses agreed on the first spending priority in 51 per cent of the households jointly spending Child Benefit, compared to 43 per cent agreement in households where the wife spends that money.

7.5 Child Benefit, Financial Management Systems and Spending Priorities

Differences in spending priorities are particularly relevant to public policy in families with dependent children. Questions on the control and use of Child Benefit offer an opportunity to examine variation among households. A second set of questions on the proposed use of an increment of £20 weekly to a household allows consideration to be extended to the different priorities of husband and wives in families with young children.

First, the use of Child Benefit is considered. Figure 7.6 looks at who decides on how Child Benefit will be spent and then at the use made of that income. Only one set of responses, that of the household manager, is available. When households are categorised based on how they manage their finances, the pervasive nature of husband control in an allowance system becomes apparent. Women are less likely than in any of the other categories to decide on the use of Child Benefit. Women's control over Child Benefit is greatest in households which manage their finances jointly.

The use made of Child Benefit is also distinctive to the various management systems. Where one person, usually the wife, is the sole manager (as in whole wage and allowance systems) the tendency is to use the money for general housekeeping and regular bills. In those households, the manager lacks an independent source of income, although they may have access to an allowance or a "kitty" contributed by other earners. Child Benefit tends to augment the money available from other sources to cover essential living expenses, a use fully in keeping with the objectives underlying the introduction of Child Benefit (see Lee, 1989: 277-85). Purchases of children's clothing represent a far larger share in households that make financial decisions jointly or independently. The manner in which money is channelled into, and distributed within, the household, then, does affect the spending priorities of household managers. In some arrangements, Child Benefit can be targeted for use for children's clothing or schooling; in others, day to day necessities have the first call.

A question was also asked of both spouses about how they would use a £20 weekly increase in their disposable income. Figure 7.7 gives the responses of wives, while Figure 7.8 provides husband's responses, thus allowing a separate look at the effects of the adopted financial management system by gender.

Figure 7.6 Control and Use of Child Benefit: Differences by Financial Management System

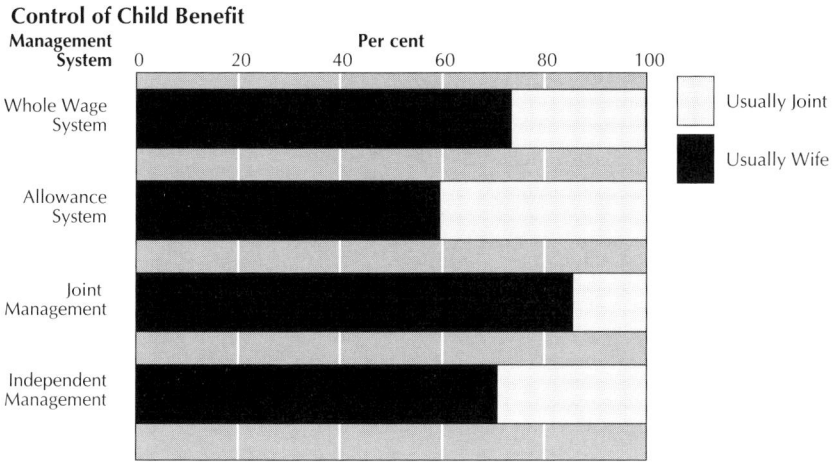

Control of Child Benefit

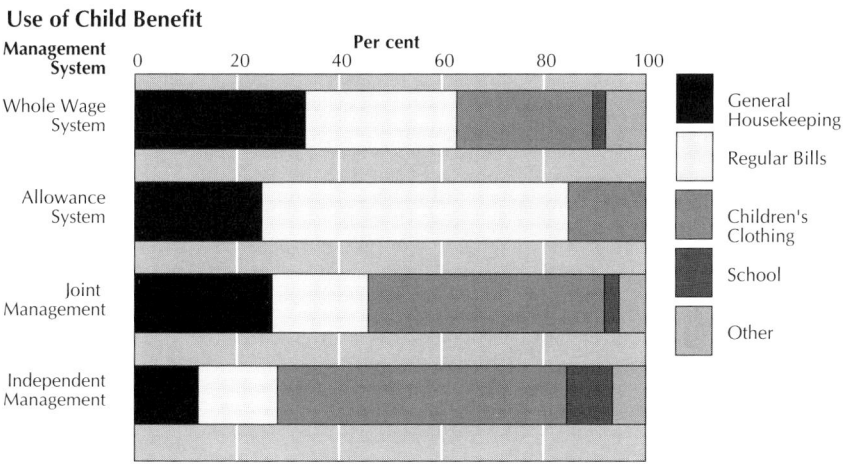

Use of Child Benefit

Source: Table D24

Figure 7.7 Wives' Priorities for Spending an Additional £20 per week[*]

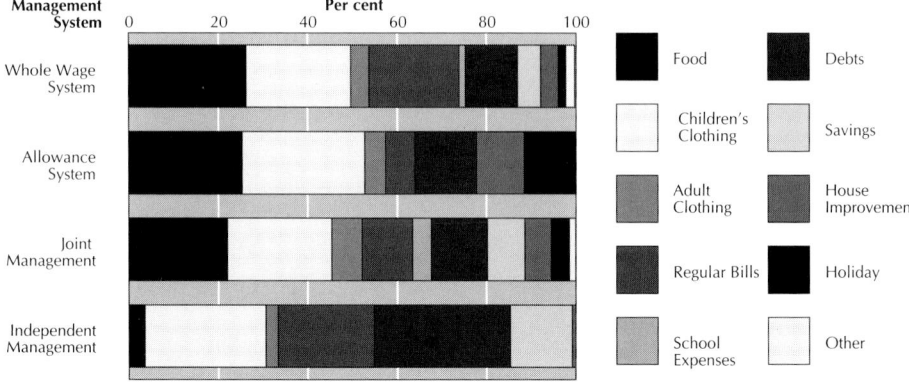

* Married couples with resident children by financial management system.
Source: Table D25

Figure 7.8 Husbands' Priorities for Spending an Additional £20 per week[*]

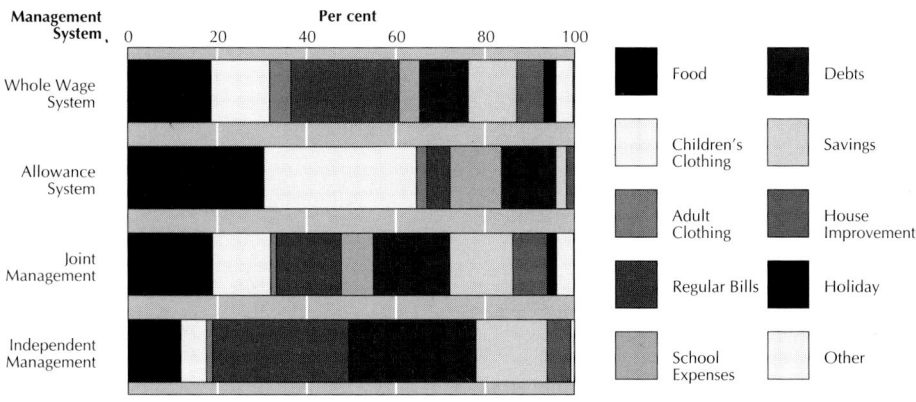

* Married couples with resident children by financial management system.
Source: Table D26

The way in which expenditure responsibility is divided, or perhaps background factors influencing the choice of system, tend to affect husbands and wives in a similar manner. This is particularly notable in the degree to which "regular bills" tend to be cited most often in the whole wage system and independently managed households, and in the greater priority afforded to debt reduction or savings in jointly and independently managed households. These are striking because they are consistent in the responses of both husbands and wives. Food is chosen as the first priority least frequently in the independent management households. A distinctive pattern for households using an allowance system is found in the choices of both spouses.

Husbands tend to cite education more frequently than do wives, perhaps reflecting traditional definitions of expenditure spheres. Similarly, husbands tend to choose the general category of "regular bills" more frequently, and also to choose "savings" as the use for the notional £20 extra per week. Women tend to give substantially greater priority to children's clothing.

7.6 Single Adult Households With Dependent Children
Focusing on married couples omits from consideration a category of households that is likely to face the maximum difficulty in making ends meet: one parent families. There were 54 households in Phase 2 with a head of household who is (a) living with one or more dependent children (aged 20 or less) and (b) who is a widow, a widower, separated, divorced, unmarried, or deserted. A profile of their income and budgetary situations can partially redress the imbalance caused by their omission from other chapters in this report.

Single adult households with dependent children are distinctive in several key respects. Income is low, day to day essentials consume a substantial proportion of total household income, dependence on social welfare payments for income is substantial, and levels of psychological distress and feelings of fatalism and powerlessness are greatly heightened. A series of comparisons between one parent households and the mass of other households can highlight the main points and the extent of the distinctiveness.

Comparisons, shown in Table 7.3, include both household characteristics and attributes of the head of household. All of the differences shown in Table

7.3 are statistically significant, except that comparing the importance of the income of the household head to the household's total income.

Table 7.3   The Circumstances of Single Parent Households in Comparative Perspective[1]

	Single Parent	Other Households	F
Food as % of Disposable Income	38.9% (16.0)	12.4% (2.5)	72.5
Household Head Income as % of Total	70.8% (24.9)	75.9% (26.2)	-
Household Head Earnings as % of Total	18.0% (27.0)	41.9% (40.5)	18.2
Average Disposable Income per Week	£173.20 (95.8)	£218.38 (161.3)	4.1
Household Head Social Welfare Recipient	90.6% (29.4)	43.7% (49.6)	47.3
GHQ Psychological Distress Score[2]	2.28 (2.5)	1.23 (2.3)	10.6
Chronic GHQ Distress Score[2]	41.5% (49.7)	18.0% (38.4)	18.4
Fatalism/Powerlessness Score[3]	17.8 (3.4)	16.3 (3.3)	9.5

Notes:

[1] Average values are used. Standard Deviations (shown in parentheses) indicate the spread around the average, and an "F" test indicates whether we can reject the null hypothesis of no difference between single and parent and other types of households.

[2] Scores range from zero to twelve based on the replies of the head of household to 12 questions. The convention is to treat scores of two or higher as indicating the presence of "chronic" psychological distress.

[3] Scores can range from four to twenty eight based on replies by the head of household to seven questions.

The strains of striving to meet family needs on low income, and without another adult in the household, are obviously considerable. In terms of the present study, however, it is not appropriate to look for a filtering effect on the part of internal management systems. The head of household is by definition the manager, main earner, and controller of family finances. Psychological distress and a sense of fatalism are predictable outcomes of such circumstances.

7.7 Conclusion

This chapter highlights some important features of the role of women's incomes in the equity with which financial decisions are made in Irish families. Women's earnings tend to be added to the general housekeeping. Women also tend to share more of their earnings than do their husbands. The proportion of women's income that is shared is affected by whether dependent children are present in the household. This is evident in the relationship between the amount of the wife's income and the percentage of that income spent on personal items. Higher earnings lead to larger percentages being spent on personal clothing and leisure only if there are no children resident. When children are present, income size is unrelated to the percentage retained for personal use.

Child Benefit provided further insight into the dynamics of family finances. In most households, Child Benefit is in the control of the wife, and is also the sole independent source of income available to her. Husband control of that money is virtually unknown. Here, joint decision-making is related to a distinctly less egalitarian financial management system. Child Benefit tends to augment what is spent on household essentials in those families in which a whole wage system prevails. This is indicative of the ambiguities of terminology and the complexity of cause and effect relationships in the study of family financial management systems.

It should be noted that there is a high degree of consensus between spouses in how to use Child Benefit and, more generally, in the choice of spending priorities. That general pattern of agreement, however, overlays some dimensions of traditional gender-based differentiation within families. Husbands tend to take responsibility for major household expenses, such as providing for housing and paying for electricity and fuel. Wives tend to be responsible for food and to be more child-oriented than husbands in their assessment of spending priorities.

CHAPTER EIGHT

Conclusions and Implications

8. Thinking about Allocation Issues

A look back at the questions raised in Chapter 1 is a logical point of departure for reflection on what can be learned from the various tables, charts, and statistics describing Irish family finances. The key questions were the degree to which spouses share their incomes, how husbands and wives divide responsibility for making household expenditures, and the extent to which consensus and equality characterise spending decisions. Answers to the three questions led to further consideration of, first, what explains why Irish families differ in those respects, and, second, whether differences in how families organise their finances can be shown to affect the well-being of individual family members.

Reasonably clear answers can be offered to the three key questions. In Irish households in 1989, it is estimated that 55 per cent of income was shared. Much of that shared income is used to pay for food and other daily necessities. On average, the weekly cost of groceries requires 59 per cent of the total shared income. A larger proportion of income is, of course, made available for the common welfare of household members through direct purchases, as when one earner purchases essential items or pays for rent or the mortgage. This look inside the "black box" of family finances thus confirms some aspects of the traditional model of sharing that underlies much of public policy. It also suggests that the assumption of sharing is not applicable to many households and that the reality is more complex than is often appreciated, particularly at the bottom and the top of the income distribution.

The prevalence of various types of financial management systems in Ireland appears to be quite different from what is reported in British studies. In the mid-1980s, whole wage systems were scarce in Britain, present in about one out of every six households. Allowance based systems were more common, but represented only one out of every four households. Half of British households used a joint management system, and one out of the twelve practised independent management (Pahl, 1983: 245-9). The results of the Irish 1989 Phase 2 survey suggest a very different pattern in Irish households. Most one-earner Irish households still follow a whole wage system. Multi-earner households tend toward an allowance-based system. Other systems of financial management are also evident. For example, in 14 per cent of Irish multi-earner households (7 per cent of all households), spouses contribute equal amounts for common use.

If one-earner and multi-earner households are combined, the division of expenditure responsibilities leads to the following classification of Irish households in 1989; one half use one person management (equivalent to whole wage management, wife control); a further 5 per cent use an allowance system (equivalent to husband control); nearly 40 per cent of households use joint management in the form of a "kitty" or allowance that is supplemented by direct purchase of some essential items by the main earner; and in one household in ten independent management prevails. Independent management means that both spouses purchase some items directly out of their own incomes and, usually, still others from a pooled household "kitty".

On balance, although full-fledged wife management, in the form of a whole wage management system, is the most common arrangement and expenditure spheres tend to fit traditional gender roles, there is scope, within a substantial proportion of Irish families, for more complex sharing of incomes and expenditure responsibilities. Insight into these arrangements is restricted in this study by the lack of detailed information on current bank accounts.

It should be noted that, in Irish households, as in other countries in which the topic has been researched, there is evidence that control and management refer to two separate aspects of financial management. Control is indexed in this report by the responses to questions inquiring about who would decide on how an unexpected medical bill would be paid and by the degree to which income is being shared. In this report the division of expenditure responsibilities indicates the type of financial management system that is being used: who takes routine responsibility for what types of purchase.

In general, the results of this study do confirm a fit between family financial management in practice and the fundamental assumption used in formulating social policy that income will be shared. While this is true of the generality of families, there are some variations and patterns worth noting, which are raised in the following sections.

8.1 Variations in Sharing and in Management Systems
Does low income, and particularly social welfare income, impose a particular financial management system? A qualified yes emerges from the survey data.

Income level, social class, labour force status and other characteristics influence the division of expenditure responsibility. There is little variation among low income households and particularly those with incomes solely derived from social welfare payments. Such families do differ, however, in the degree to which income is being shared and thus made available for spending by and on women and children. Sharing of income is most common in households at middle income levels. It is, however, distinctively low in families dependent on social welfare for their incomes. The meaning of sharing also varies considerably depending on the income level of the household. In low income households, shared income mainly accounts for expenditures on essentials such as food and fuel. On average, households receiving more than one-half of their income in the form of social welfare share less of their income than do households in the bottom income quartile. There is, however, diversity among households dependent on social welfare income.

At higher levels of income, sharing creates a pool of discretionary income that can be used for common household purposes and control over that money becomes more contentious. More elaborate, and probably more equitable in principle, forms of decision making therefore become possibilities only where both spouses have access to an income and where discretionary income is available to the household. However, the pattern of results echoes findings from studies conducted elsewhere in that indications of overall husband control are often present even in households that share both income and responsibilities. The presence of discretionary income tends to support husband control, because it makes possible the kinds of purchases that are traditionally seen as being within the husband's competence. As a result, higher levels of household income do not predictably promote greater equality in financial decision-making.

Wife management, by contrast, is most likely to be found at low levels of household income, where income is in the form of social welfare payments, and in farm households. Among middle class families (social classes 1 and 2), wives' employment promotes independent management of family finances. There is no clear effect from a wife's employment on financial decision-making in other social classes.

Husband control, to the extent that it can be distinguished in this study, therefore tends to be prevalent in situations where either very little or a great deal of income is being shared. Husband control in low income families can take the form of sole access to income and sole responsibility for purchases.

To conclude, Irish households tend to share income and to share responsibilities for expenditure. But the potential for sharing expenditure responsibility is conditional to a large extent upon income sharing. Joint and independent management tends, therefore, to be most common at higher income levels and in middle class households.

Does access to an independent income lead to more equitable participation in financial decisions? Wives' earnings tend to be added to the general housekeeping and wives also tend to share more of their earnings than do husbands. The proportion of wives' income that is shared is affected by whether there are dependent children present in the household. This is evident in the relationship between the amount of the wife's income and the percentage of that income spent on personal items. Higher earnings lead to larger percentages being spent on personal clothing and leisure only if there are no children resident. When children are present, income size is unrelated to the percentage retained for personal use.

8.2 Aspects of Financial Control and Management

Some important features of financial decision-making in Irish households are described in the report. One is the extent to which spouses agree on how they make decisions. The level of agreement is both substantial and tends, where the choice is available, to characterise important decisions as being made jointly. There remains a substantial proportion of households in which it is clear that the husband has the dominant say in making financial decisions. Disagreement on financial matters is most common in households practising independent management, as indexed by the way expenditure responsibilities are divided. While the scope for disagreement is arguably greatest among that group, the extent of chronic disputes over financial matters (as indicated by the percentage of households disagreeing on a multiplicity of items) tends to be lower than in other households.

The use of Child Benefit provides further insight into the dynamics of finances and financial decision-making. If we look at all couples receiving Child Benefit, we find that in 58 per cent of couples women have no other direct source of income; in 10 per cent women have income in their own right but it is smaller than the Child Benefit they receive. This leaves 32 per cent of all couples in which women receive income that exceeds what the State currently provides as Child Benefit. However, in the bottom two income quintiles, only 15 per cent of women have access to a form of income greater than Child Benefit.

This study lacks the evidence to determine if Child Benefit is more likely than other forms of income to be spent on children. But the amount families receive as Child Benefit payments are clearly adding to the total amount being spent on raising children. In higher income households, this tends to be through direct expenses such as clothing. Thus, even at the highest income levels, the survey responses indicate that Child Benefit is targeted to meet the costs of children. The pattern in low income households tends to be for Child Benefit to be channelled indirectly toward the costs of children, by assisting the parents in providing basic household essentials, like food, fuel and housing. Generally, then, families spend Child Benefit in the manner that, based on their circumstances, is most advantageous to children. Child Benefit tends to augment what is spent on household essentials in those families in which the whole wage management system prevails.

In assessing the policy issues surrounding Child Benefit, it is relevant that husband control of Child Benefit is virtually unknown. Joint decision-making in this arena is rare, but when present is related to a distinctly less egalitarian financial management system.

In the use of Child Benefit and in the choice of spending priorities, there is a substantial degree of agreement between spouses. That general pattern of agreement, however, overlays some dimensions of traditional gender-based differentiation within families. Husbands tend to take responsibility for major household expenses, such as providing for housing and paying for electricity and fuel. Wives tend to be responsible for food and to be more child-oriented than husbands in their assessment of spending priorities.

Overall, the findings tend to confirm what British and North American studies indicate, despite the greater resilience of whole wage and allowance based systems in this country. The gist of international research is well summarised by Morris:

> spending decisions involving large amounts of money are taken by men, whilst day-to-day budgeting tends to be the responsibility of women ... There are a number of ways in which position in the labour market

comes to influence a household's financial arrangements. Simply put, these largely relate to size and source of income. The larger the income the more involvement the man has in household financial affairs, arguably because of the greater capacity for spending in large amounts - a characteristically male preserve. The smaller the income the closer total income is to the level required for minimal domestic needs and the more likely it is to be managed by the woman. This is especially true in cases of benefit dependence. Women's earnings at the lower level do little to affect these patterns ... though at a higher level of status and income women's employment brings a greater probability that there will be some shared element in the overall management of finances, (1990: 193-4).

This is a reasonable characterisation of the patterns reported for Irish households in Chapters 3 to 7.

8.3 Consequences of Financial Management Systems

The equity with which members of households enjoy access to personal spending money and to leisure is related to the financial management system being used. The division of personal expenditure and of access to leisure tends to favour husbands in all but independently managed households. Overall, however, the similarities between spouses in any category or at any level of income sharing tend to outweigh the differences.

The consequences of how household finances are managed are quite significant for the well-being of individual members. Access to leisure and to personal spending money is used in this report to indicate the material inequalities that are present. There are also implications for the psychological well-being of family members. Scores of psychological distress and of fatalism are higher for wives when low amounts of income are being shared. The absolute amount that is shared appears to be more consequential in these terms than the total amount of income flowing into the household. That is, the amount of money being shared is a better predictor of the levels of psychological distress and the feelings of fatalism or powerlessness experienced by spouses than is total household disposable income. The links are complex and only partially established at this stage. But the evidence that financial management systems matter for the lives of people living in Irish households is strong. As in other countries, women tend to have greater access to personal spending money if they have an independent source of income. A whole wage system may work to women's advantage in some households. At low incomes, for example, inequity in access to shared income is at its maximum, but where the wife does have access, it is to higher amounts, on average, than for husbands. Whole wage or one person management does involve a price for the manager: full responsibility for making ends meet on a day to day basis.

Along with these practical consequences, financial management systems are involved in the complex relationships between family circumstances and psychological well-being. The essential linkage in that relationship can, however, be stated with confidence, opening a new area for research on family finances and management systems. In Ireland, standard measures of psychological distress and feelings of fatalism are linked to the extent of income sharing and the financial management system used by a household. These effects are present for both husbands and wives, but tend to be stronger in the case of wives.

The concluding question is whether the survey results lend credence to claims that substantial numbers of women and children live in "hidden poverty", hidden because conventional studies of poverty attribute a household's income to all of its members. Here, the answer is necessarily speculative because the available evidence is so indirect: the consensus between spouses on financial matters such as spending priorities, the extent of income sharing, and the moderate inequalities in access to leisure. But it is difficult to reconcile this pattern of differences with the existence of a significant reservoir of individual poverty hidden among the notional affluence of households. In other words, it is unlikely that Irish women and children in households above conventional poverty lines live in conditions comparable to those experienced by women and children in households below those lines. The two categories of households that qualify as exceptions are those in which Child Benefit is spent jointly or in which the husband is the main earner and the household manager - husband control indeed.

Nevertheless, the presence of clear gender inequality is not in dispute. It is manifest in the division between husbands and wives of expenditure responsibilities, the power to make major financial decisions (as indexed by the question on how an emergency expense would be met), and in the various measures of access to leisure and personal spending money.

However, the resulting differences in the standards of living experienced by husbands, on the one hand, and wives and children, on the other, are not sufficient to warrant a claim that poverty studies based on individuals rather than households will uncover a massive lode of "hidden poverty".

Appendix A: Data Linkage , Reweighting and Validation

When sample surveys are carried out it is frequently necessary to reweight the data collected to eliminate non-random bias and thus ensure that the results are representative of the population as a whole. This is usually carried out by so-called ratio weighting techniques, which compare the sample and the population from which it is drawn along various dimensions of a weighting matrix and correct for any over- or under-representation.

In the present instance, it is necessary to consider the interviews obtained in Phases 1 and 2 for each household simultaneously. This means that we are effectively linking data collected in two separate sample surveys and so must develop a reweighting system to ensure the representativeness of the resultant data set. A particular complication arises in the study because only a sub-sample of households which were successfully interviewed in Phase 1 were selected for inclusion in Phase 2. Furthermore, as previously noted, the non-response rate was 28 per cent. It is therefore necessary to adjust for any non-random bias in both (a) the differential selection probabilities of households for inclusion in the Phase 2 target sample and (b) the differential response rates among households in that sample. The differential selection probabilities arise because all households in the lowest quartile of the Phase 1 income distribution were selected for inclusion in the second phase target sample along with a further 500 households selected at random from the remaining 2,502 households in the top three quartiles. This meant that households in the lowest quartile each had a selection probability of unity, compared with a selection probability of 0.2 for those households in the top three quartiles.

Further, it was necessary to take into account the non-random biases inherent in the Phase 1 achieved sample, along the same lines as was implemented in Callan *et al*, (1989). Therefore, a two stage reweighting procedure was developed for use with the effective Phase 2 sample. In the first stage of this reweighting, adjustment was made for the differential selection and response probabilities in the effective Phase 2 sample. This was done using a four dimensional weighting matrix based on: (a) urban/rural location; (b) number of adults in the household; (c) labour force status of head of household; and (d) Phase 1 income quartile. This stage of reweighting ensured that the Phase 2 sample of 918 households was grossed up in such a way as to be representative of the Phase 1 effective sample of 3,286 households. In practice, the Phase 1 sample is the "population" from which the Phase 2 sample was drawn. The second stage of the reweighting procedure ensures that the 3,286 households of Phase 1 were themselves representative of the national population of private households in 1987 (the base year in which the panel was initially selected). This latter weight was based on a four dimensional matrix of: (a) urban/rural location of household; (b) number of adults in the household; (c) occupation of head of household; (d) age of head of household. This second stage weighting matrix was derived from the 1986 Labour Force Survey. This meant that by the end of the second stage of reweighting, the 918 cases in the effective sample of Phase 2 represented the 1,007,300 households in the 1986 Labour Force Survey. These reweighting data differ from their unweighted counterparts in that they have the same structure as the national population along critical, social and demographic dimensions. The dimensions of these matrices are felt to be the key determinants of household income.

A further weighting complication arises due to the longitudinal quality of the data. A weight must be assigned to each of the 49 new households generated in Ireland by former residents of the original panel's households. However, for these households created by members of the 1987 sample there is no external frame of reference for new household generation over the period in question on which to make comparisons. The total population of new households generated is not known, nor are any of their characteristics. Thus, we cannot gross the new households up to a population figure. Under such circumstances there are two options for their reweighting. First, each new household can be given the average weight of its "parent" household. Secondly, each new household can be given the average weight of all other households in the effective Phase 2 sample. This average weight is unity. The latter option was selected.[1]

Having undertaken such a complex reweighting procedure it is obviously prudent to test for the representativeness of the resulting data. In survey research this is normally done by comparing reweighted survey results with published census and other authoritative sources. In a longitudinal study, however, even such an apparently straightforward procedure becomes more complex. There are two ways of assessing the efficacy of the reweighting procedure. First, the distribution of key variables extracted from the reweighted Phase 2 sample of 918 households can be compared with those published by the Central Statistics Office (CSO) for the population as a whole. Secondly, we can contrast the distribution of some key variables in 1987, based on the full Phase 1 sample of 3,286 cases, with the comparable distribution derived from the much smaller Phase 2 sample of 918 households using Phase 2 weights. The reweighted results from the two samples should not be significantly different provided the weighting procedure works well. Thus, the reweighted Phase 2 results are compared with data published by the CSO on all households. The reweighted Phase 2 sample is not representative of the population of households in 1989. Rather, it is representative of the characteristics of 1987 households that survived into 1989. Although this means that there will not be an exact coincidence between CSO and ESRI reweighted data, they should be very similar. Such differences as do exist can be attributed to two factors: (i) the natural dynamics of the population over the period 1987 to 1989 and (ii) differences in methodologies, definitions, measurement and sampling error.

Table A1 compares the distribution of the principal economic status of all persons aged 15 years and over as derived from the 1989 round of the survey with that published from the 1986 Census. Principal economic status is a particularly apt point of comparison because it is a key determinant of a household's financial circumstances. Household income and the ratio of income-to-needs are primarily a function of the number of

---

[1] A conventional precaution when using multi-stage clustered samples is to increase the width of confidence intervals around any estimates of population characteristics by a factor of about 1.5 over what would occur in pure random sampling (see Moser and Kalton, 1972: pp. 200-209). However, the emphasis in this report is on examining relationships between variables rather than on establishing precise point estimates.

economically active and/or dependent persons within the household. The sample and 1986 population figures are quite similar for both males and females.

Table A2 presents a classification of the population by age and sex from the 1986 Census and from the Phase 2 sample. The national situation is 1986 is reflected in the ESRI sample in Phase 2 of the Survey. It is worth noting that the sample had a slightly higher percentage of both males and females in the 65-74 age group than in the Census. The ESRI's survey is based on the population in private households and specifically excludes the institutionalised population, most of whom are in this upper age category. We would thus expect the ESRI sample to be below the national levels in these upper age cohorts. The fact that the sample has a slightly higher than expected percentage in these older age cohorts tends to point, at least in part, to an ageing of the sample between the two phases. Also, Tables A1 and A2 do not consider the new households set up by people in the lower age categories and among whom birth rates would be highest. These new households would tend to depress the average age of the population. Their exclusion, therefore, brings the mean age of persons in the sample to slightly above the national average. The average age of household members from the Phase 1 sample of 1987 was 30.3 years. The average age of members from households that survived into the second phase sample was 31.6 years.

Table A1   Persons Aged 15 Years and Over Classified by Principal Economic Status and Sex

Principal Economic Status	ESRI Survey, Phase Two		Census 1986	
	Males	Females	Males	Females
	Per Cent		Per Cent	
At Work	56.8	29.1	59.6	27.5
Unemployed	12.4	2.0	12.3	3.3
First Job Seeker	1.9	1.2	2.1	1.3
Student	9.7	9.7	9.8	9.7
Home Duties	0.0	52.3	0.0	51.4
Other	19.2	5.6	16.2	6.7
Total	**100.0**	**99.9**	**100.0**	**99.9**
% of all persons persons 15 +	**49.4**	**50.6**	**49.4**	**50.5**

Source: Census 1986, Summary Population Report - 2nd Series, CSO November 1989, Table C p.14. ESRI Survey, Spring 1989. (ESRI data based on "Surviving" Phase 1 households only).

Appendix A

Table A2   Persons Classified by Age Group and Sex Based on ESRI Survey and Census 1986

Age Group (years)	ESRI Survey, Phase Two		Census 1986	
	Males	Females	Males	Females
	Per Cent		Per Cent	
0 - 4	8.8	9.2	9.4	8.9
5 - 14	22.4	21.5	20.3	19.3
15 - 24	15.1	13.2	17.7	17.1
25 - 34	13.0	14.2	14.2	14.1
35 - 44	12.4	11.9	12.1	11.7
45 - 54	9.4	8.3	8.9	8.5
55 - 64	8.1	8.6	7.8	8.2
65 - 74	8.5	8.8	6.3	7.3
75 +	2.3	4.2	3.2	4.9
Total	**100.0**	**99.9**	**100.0**	**100.0**

Source: Census 1986, Summary Population Report, Central Statistics Office, November 1987, Tables 4B and 4C pp 6-7; ESRI Lifestyles Survey, Phase 2, Spring 1989. (ESRI data based on "Surviving" Phase 1 households only).

The incidence of social welfare transfers is of particular relevance to any study of income and poverty. Table A3 compares Phase 2 survey estimates with Department of Social Welfare figures on the percentage of the population in receipt of social welfare payments and the breakdown of recipients by type. Because there are flows of recipients into and out of the system over even short periods of time, the Department's figures are shown in relation to 31 December 1988 and also 31 December 1989. These two points provide a baseline for incidence levels in the period March to May 1989, to which the survey makes reference. The table also presents an estimated distribution of payment types from the ESRI survey. From these figures we can see that Department of Social Welfare statistics suggest that approximately 20 per cent of the population was in receipt of social welfare payments in 1989. This compares with an estimated figure of 19 per cent from the ESRI Survey. From the breakdown of recipients by type of payment, we can see that there is strong agreement between the figures published by the Department and survey estimates. For example, the Departmental statistics suggest that 31 per cent of social welfare recipients receive unemployment payments (benefits and assistance); the comparable survey estimate is 30 per cent. The greatest discrepancy is for pensions. Some of the discrepancy for individual schemes may be attributable to confusion by respondents as to precisely which pension type they receive. From Departmental figures it appears that approximately 48 per cent of all social welfare recipients were in receipt of one of these three pensions (old age pension, retirement pension, widow's pension) at the end of 1989. This compares with an estimate of 51 per cent in the sample.

The distributions in Tables A1, A2, and A3 therefore offer substantial reassurance about the status of the reweighted data. Comparisons to population characteristics from available published statistics validate the representativeness of the data set.

Table A3   Percentage Breakdown of Social Welfare Recipients by Payment Type Based on Social Welfare Statistics (a,b) and ESRI Survey Data (c)

	(a)	(b)	(c)
	Dept. Social Welfare Statistics		**ESRI Survey**
	December 31, 1988	**December 31, 1989**	**March-May,1989**
	Per Cent		**Per Cent**
Old Age Pension [1]	27.2	27.4	38.0
Retirement Pension	5.7	6.3	2.5
Widow's Pensions [1,2]	13.9	14.4	10.5
Single Woman's Allowance	0.3	0.3	0.2
Disability Benefit [3]	8.7	8.0	6.0
Invalidity Pension	4.0	4.3	5.2
Disablement Benefit	1.0	1.0	1.3
Injury Benefit	0.1	0.1	0.1
Maternity Benefit	0.5	0.5	0.6
Unemployment Benefit	10.2	8.6	9.9
Unemployment Assistance [4]	21.6	22.0	20.1
Orphan's Pension [1]	0.1	0.1	0.0
Deserted Wife's Payment [1]	1.9	2.1	2.4
Unmarried Mother's Allowance	2.1	2.3	1.3
Prisoner Wife's Allowance	0.0	0.0	0.0
Rent Allowance	1.6	1.6	-
Supplementary Welfare Allowance	0.7	0.8	1.0
Family Income Support	0.2	0.2	0.9
Total	**100.0**	**100.0**	**100.0**
	(N=726,410)	(N=715,540)	(N=918 hsds.)
Receipts as % of total population	**20.5%**	**20.4%**	**19.1%**

Source: Statistical Information on Social Welfare Services, 1988 and 1989, Department of Social Welfare, 1989 and 1990. ESRI Survey on Lifestyles and State Services, Phase Two, 1989.

Notes: (1) Contributory and Non Contributory
    (2) Includes 108 widowers in 1989; 466 Death Benefit Pensions in 1988 and 463 Death Benefit Pensions in 1989
    (3) Includes 1,044 Interim Disability Benefit in 1988 and 1,653 Interim Disability Benefit in 1989.
    (4) Includes Small Holders Allowance

Appendix A

Still, in view of the complexity of the reweighted procedure it is prudent to check the effects further. This can be done by comparing a key variable, such as 1987 household income as estimated from the full Phase 1 data set of 3,286 households, with the Phase 2 data, using the weights created specifically for each phase. Since the latter sample of 918 "old" households is effectively a sub-sample of the Phase 1 sample, the full set of Phase 1 households serves as an external frame of reference (population figures) against which to compare the figures derived from a sub-sample of the "population" using a new weighting system. Table A4 reports the mean household income in 1987 based on (a) the 3,294 cases of Phase 1 and (b) the 918 cases of Phase 2 using the Phase 2 weights. The estimates are very similar and also compare well with the average household income figure of £200.96 obtained by the Central Statistics Office from its 1987 Household Budget Survey. The table also shows the breakdown of average household income into its main components: earnings, social welfare income, and "other" income. There is virtually no difference in the percentage figures derived using the different estimation bases. For further details see Callan, Nolan et al., 1989: Chapter 4; and Williams and Whelan, 1994.

Table A4 Average Household Income in 1987 and the Average Percentage Breakdown of that Income into Labour, Social Welfare and "Other" Elements for the 1987 Population of Households: (a) full Phase 1 Sample and (b) 918 Cases of the Phase 2 Sample.

	(a) From 3,296 Cases of Phase 1 Sample and Phase 1 Weights	(b) From 918 Cases of Phase 2 Sample and Phase 2 Weights
Average Household Income	IR£ 198.00	IR£ 201.44
Average percentage of household income accounted for by:	**Per Cent**	**Per Cent**
Labour Income	0.55	0.56
Social Welfare	0.37	0.36
"Other" Income	0.08	0.08
Total	100.00	100.00

Appendix B: Social Class Tables

Table B1   Social Class of Heads of Household and All Persons: ERSI Phase 2 Survey and 1986 Census of Population

Social Class	ESRI Survey Phase 2		Census of Population, 1986
	HOH	All Persons	All Persons
	Per Cent		Per Cent
Higher professional	10.7	10.7	9.9
Lower professional	12.3	13.1	14.1
Other non-manual	16.2	16.5	17.5
Skilled manual	25.6	27.5	22.8
Semi-skilled manual	19.2	18.7	15.4
Unskilled manual	12.4	11.8	10.2
Unknown	3.7	1.9	10.1
Total	100.0	100.0	100.0

Table B2 Average Head of Household Income by Social Class

Social Class	Average Head of Household Income	Standard Deviation	N
	IR £		
Higher professional	241.21	(205.9)	104
Lower professional	208.54	(102.3)	119
Other non-manual	153.93	(96.1)	156
Skilled manual	142.62	(81.8)	147
Semi-skilled manual	111.62	(70.9)	186
Unskilled manual	85.42	(34.0)	120
Unknown	81.20	(44.1)	35
Total	147.81	(111.55)	867

Appendix C

Appendix C: Multiple Regression Analysis and Psychological Stress

Multiple regression analysis can be used to establish the degree to which allocation-related variables can predict psychological health. Psychological distress is measured by the widely used 12 item General Health Questionnaire (GHQ) scale, as shown in Table C1.

Table C1 General Health Questionnaire (GHQ) Items

1.	Been feeling unhappy and depressed?
2.	Felt capable of making decisions about things?
3.	Felt that you couldn't overcome your difficulties?
4.	Been feeling reasonably happy all things considered?
5.	Been able to face up to your problems?
6.	Been thinking of yourself as a worthless person?
7.	Felt able to enjoy your day to day activities?
8.	Lost much sleep over worry?
9.	Felt that you are playing a useful part in things?
10.	Felt constantly under strain?
11.	Been able to concentrate on what you are doing?
12.	Been losing confidence in yourself.

Source: Whelan *et al*, 1991:19

As can be seen in Table C1 the GHQ items are made up of six positive and six negative items. The scoring system for these items is shown in Table C2. The alpha (reliability) coefficient for the GHQ scale in the ESRI data is 0.82

Table C2 General Health Questionnaire Scoring

Negative Items Scoring (1, 2, 5, 7, 8, 10)	Not at All	No More Than Usual	Rather More Than Usual	Much More Than Usual
(GHQ) Score	0	0	1	1
Positive Items Scoring (3, 4, 6, 9, 11, 12)	More So Than Usual	Same As Usual	Less So Than Usual	Much Less Than Usual
(GHQ) Score	0	0	1	1

Source: Whelan *et al*, 1991:19

Fatalism is measured on a six item scale on which low scores indicate a feeling of "mastery" and high scores feelings of fatalism or powerlessness. These are shown in Table C3.

Table C3 Fatalism/Mastery Items

1.	I can do just about anything I set my mind to.
2.	I have little control over the things that happen to me.
3.	What happens in the future depends on me.
4.	I often feel helpless in dealing with the problems of life.
5.	Sometimes I feel I am being pushed around in life.
6.	There is really no way I can solve some of the problems I have.

Source: Whelan *et al*, 1991:112

The alpha coefficient for this set of items is 0.68. The correlation between fatalism and the GHQ score is 0.40. When we correct for attenuation of the correlation due to measurement error, the correlation rises to 0.52. Thus, a relationship exists between these variables.

The following paragraphs help to explain the variables used in the multiple regression analysis and the technique itself. First, how are the predictor variables measured? Social class is treated as an ordinal variable using the six category CSO scale (see Chapter 5 of this report). Welfare reliance is a dichotomy, with a value of one for households that receive more than half of their total income from social welfare payments. The amount of shared income is a continuous variable expressed in pounds per week. The division of expenditure responsibility is measured by three "dummy variables". That is, households using a financial management system are scored one on the appropriate dummy variable and other households are assigned a score of zero. Regression analysis requires that one of the four categories be omitted from the equations: the absent category is "the whole wage system"("one person management").

Secondly, what indicates whether an explanatory variable is important? The relative importance as predictors for social class, welfare reliance, and shared incomes can be seen from the corresponding beta coefficients (standardised regression coefficient) presented in Tables C4 and C5. Interpretation is more complex for the impact of financial management systems. While each "dummy variable" has a beta weight indicating the effect on the criterion of using that financial management system, the salient issue here is their combined impact, as registered in the change to the R^2 statistic shown at the bottom of each column in the tables.

The key concern, then, is whether the amount being shared and the three "dummy variables" explain a statistically significant percentage of the variation in the criterion

Appendix C

beyond that attributable to social class and social welfare status.[1] The relevant evidence from multiple regression analysis is presented in Table C4 for psychological distress and in Table C5 for fatalism. Each column in the tables represents the results of a predictive equation. The first equation to the left of a series of three equations provides the baseline: what social class and welfare status predict about the psychological criteria. For wives, those two variables have an R2 of 0.131, which means that they explain 13.1 per cent of the variation in psychological distress. The main findings of the regression analysis are presented in chapter 6 of this report.

Table C4   Multiple Regression Results: The Impact of Social Class, Welfare Status, Income Sharing, and Expenditure Responsibility on Psychological Distress[1]

	Wife			Husband		
	(i)	(ii)	(iii)	(i)	(ii)	(iii)
Social Class	0.09*	0.07*	0.10*	0.09*	0.08	0.11**
Welfare Income	0.32**	0.29**	0.33**	0.30**	0.27**	0.32**
Shared Income		-0.09*			- 0.08	
Expenditure Responsibility [4]			0.08*			0.14*
Expenditure Responsibility [2]			0.08*			0.06
Expenditure Responsibility [3]			0.05			0.06
R^2	0.131	0.136	0.142	0.122	0.126	0.140
F	42.6	29.8	18.8	39.3	27.2	6.60
N	569	569	569	569	569	569

* P < .05

** P < .01

No asterisk = not significant

1 Social class measured as an ordinal variable using the six category CSO scale (see Chapter 5 of this report). Welfare income is a dichotomy, with a value of one for households receiving income more than one half of their income from social welfare, shared income is the amount shared weekly, as reported by the household manager.
2 Allowance System   ) Note: Regression analysis requires that one of the four categories
3 Joint Management   ) be omitted from the equations: the absent category is "the
4 Independent Management) whole wage system" ("one person management").
Note: (i), (ii) and (iii) identify regression equations. Three predictive equations were tested for wives and then repeated for the husbands. In Equation (i), only the effects of social welfare income are included; Equation (ii) adds the extent of shared income to the prediction; and finally in Equation (iii) the financial management system being used is added to the above factors.

[1] For those familiar with multiple regression and the general linear model on which it is based, the amount of money being shared is in practice the interaction effect created by multiplying household disposable income by the percentage of income shared.

Table C5   Multiple Regression Results: The Impact of Social Class, Welfare Status, Income, and Expenditure Responsibility on Fatalism[1]

	Wife			Husband		
	(i)	(ii)	(iii)	(i)	(ii)	(iii)
Social Class	0.19**	0.17**	0.21**	0.14**	0.14**	0.15**
Welfare Income	0.25**	0.19*	0.25**	0.30**	0.29**	0.30**
Shared Income		0.13**			- 0.03	
Expenditure Responsibility [4]			0.08*			0.04
Expenditure Responsibility [2]			0.15**			0.14**
Expenditure Responsibility [3]			-0.00			0.04
R^2	0.137	0.149	0.164	0.143	0.144	0.163
F	45.1	331	22.2	475	317	27.2
N	569	569	569	569	569	569

* $P < .05$

** $P < .01$

No asterisk = not significant

1   Social classes measured as an ordinal variable using the six category CSO scale (see Chapter 5 of this report). Welfare income is a dichotomy, with a value of one for households receiving income more than one half of their income from social welfare, shared income is the amount shared weekly, as reported by the household manager.

2   Allowance System   ) Note: Regression analysis requires that one of the four categories

3   Joint Management   ) be omitted from the equations: the absent category is "the

4   Independent Management) whole wage system" ("one person management").

Note: (i), (ii) and (iii) identify regression equations. Three predictive equations were tested for wives and then repeated for the husbands. In Equation (i), only the effects of social welfare income are included; Equation (ii) adds the extent of shared income to the prediction; and finally in Equation (iii) the financial management system being used is added to the above factors.

The amount of income being shared also enhances the explained variances in feelings of fatalism and appears, both for husbands and wives, to be a more important predictor than income level itself. How expenditure responsibilities are divided again adds modestly, but to a statistically significant degree, to the explained variance (generally about 2 per cent). The positive values for coefficients representing the three dummy variables indicate that households in those categories tend to score higher on the fatalism scale than do households in the omitted category (whole system management).

Appendix C

Caution is warranted on several grounds. First, statistically significant effects are ones in which there is reassurance that the result is not due to random factors that affect the particular set of persons or households included in the study. Secondly, although statistically significant, the amount of variation in psychological distress attributable to the degree of financial management systems is small: generally a few percentages of the total variation. The relationship is stronger when fatalism/powerlessness is the criterion. Thirdly, as noted in Chapter 2, the Phase 2 panel survey data have been heavily reweighted to correct for low participation on both Phases 1 and 2 by certain types of households and the use of a sub-sample of households. Fourthly, psychological distress is related to income level, social class, gender, employment status and other factors in a complex but coherent manner. (Whelan *et al*, 1991). The claims of an independent influence from income sharing and financial management system made here are net of the effects of social class, welfare reliance, and income level. Fifthly, even when restricted to the arena of financial management the effects on psychological health require further elaboration before they are adequately understood. Earlier in the report (Chapter 5) it emerged that sharing of income is highest among middle income families. Those with the highest and lowest incomes share the least.[2]

---

[2] The bivariate correlation between sharing and psychological distress is moderately strong and negative in direction. To illustrate the nature of the relationship, if the four quartile values of income sharing are used the following average GHQ scores are found for wives in each quartile: 1st, 1.49; 2nd, 1.39; 3rd, 0.98; 4th, 0.52. A standard measure of the strength of that relationship, Eta is 0.178. Total household disposable income is not correlated with the percentage that is shared (r=0.028). However, the correlation between disposable income and the amount that is shared is substantial, 0.61. This poses potential problems of multicollinearity if the variables are used as predictors in the same equation and thus puts some roadblocks in front of a straightforward interpretation of the result.

Appendix D: Tables Supporting Charts

Table D1 Financial Management Systems : One-Earner Households

	Number of Households	Per Cent of Households
Whole Wage / Wife Control	219	73.5
Whole Wage / Husband Control	14	4.7
Allowance for All Expenses	37	12.4
Allowance for "Most" Expenses	28	9.4
Total	**298[1]**	**100.00**

[1] Two of the 300 one-earner households did not answer the relevant question.

Table D2 Financial Management Systems in Ireland

	All Households	All Married Couples
	Per Cent	Per Cent
One Adult Households	19	NA
One Earner Households	**33.7**	**49.9**
System 1 : Whole Wage/Wife Control		36.7
System 2 : Whole Wage/Husband Control		2.3
System 3 : Allowance for All Expenses		6.2
System 4 : Allowance for Most Expenses		4.7
Multi-Earner Households	**46.6**	**49.8**
System 5 : Main Earner Shares more than 75%		10.2
System 6 : Main Earner Shares less than 75%		10.1
System 7 : Matched Contributions		6.7
System 8 : Joint Sharing more than 75%		8.9
System 9 : Main Earner more than 75% / Second earner less than 75%		7.0
System 10: Both Earners less than 75%		6.9
Total	**100.00** (N=967)	**100.0** (N=956)

Percentages may not sum exactly to 100 per cent due to rounding

Appendix D

Table D3 Spheres of Expenditure Responsibility[1]

How are the following items usually paid for?						
	Household Manager from "Kitty"	Household Manager from Own Income	Directly by Main Earner	Other Member	Total	
Items			**Per cent**			
Food	92.0	2.8	5.2	0.0	100%	(623)
Rent/mortgage	62.7	3.4	33.6	0.3	100%	(422)
ESB	69.4	2.3	27.8	0.4	100%	(614)
Coal or gas	72.5	1.9	25.1	0.5	100%	(616)
Wife's clothes	78.6	6.7	13.7	1.0	100%	(610)
Husband's clothes	59.2	2.0	38.1	0.7	100%	(608)
Child's clothes	78.6	5.7	13.7	2.0	100%	(437)
School expenses	73.6	3.7	22.3	0.4	100%	(351)
Child's recreation	82.6	2.5	14.0	0.9	100%	(387)
Child's money	75.2	3.1	20.9	0.8	100%	(310)

[1] Percentages exclude households for which an item of expenditure is not applicable, as where a home is owned outright or where dependent children are not present. Parentheses indicate the number of households included in each preceding percentage.

Table D4 Disagreements in Financial Assessments

	Frequency	Per cent
None	478	78.7
One	96	15.7
Two	18	3.0
Three	11	1.8
Four	4	0.7
Five	1	0.1
Total	**608**	**100.0**

Table D5   Average Amounts of Personal Spending Money by Income Quintile: (based on persons reporting some money available)[1]

Quintile	Wife	Husband	Both Spouses
	£	£	£
Bottom	8.52	4.70	12.72
	(7.3)	(6.2)	(9.6)
2nd	9.33	9.23	19.08
	(6.0)	(10.6)	(14.6)
3rd	9.92	13.29	22.59
	(6.1)	(11.0)	(13.4)
4th	14.44	13.88	24.75
	(15.4)	(9.8)	(18.9)
Top	16.95	18.45	34.96
	(15.5)	(16.7)	(30.4)
	N=375	N=583	N=493

[1] Parentheses contain standard deviations. Averages and standard deviations refer only to those households in which personal spending money is reported. The totals for both spouses refer to households in which either or both spouses report access to regular personal spending money.

Key: Income quintiles group households on the basis of their total disposable incomes:

Bottom quintile:	Lowest	-	£127.94 per week
2nd quintile:	£127.95	-	£185.94 per week
3rd quintile:	£185.95	-	£247.27 per week
4th quintile:	£247.28	-	£329.42 per week
Top quintile:	£329.43	-	highest per week

Appendix D

Table D6 Main Reasons for Not Having an Afternoon/Evening Out?

Reason Indicated	Wife	Husband
No desire to	34.8	43.0
Full social life in other ways	5.1	1.6
Not enough money	41.6	43.8
Cannot leave children	10.4	2.9
Ill	2.4	3.4
Other obligations	5.6	5.5
Total	**100%**	**100%**
	(N=256)	(N=217)

Table D7 Percentage of Husbands and Wives with Personal Spending Money By Income Quintile

Household Income Quintile	Husbands	Wives
Bottom	51.7%	35.3%
2nd	69.9%	53.1%
3rd	80.7%	52.1%
4th	83.5%	71.4%
Top	93.5%	86.7%
	(N=616)	(N=621)

Key: Income quintiles group households on the basis of their total disposable incomes:
Bottom quintile: Lowest   -   £127.94 per week
2nd quintile: £127.95   -   £185.94 per week
3rd quintile: £185.95   -   £247.27 per week
4th quintile: £247.28   -   £329.42 per week
Top quintile: £329.43   -   highest per week

Table D8 Financial Management Systems: Differences by Income Quintiles

Household Income	Whole Wage System	Allowance System	Joint Management	Independent Management	Total[1]
		Per Cent			
Bottom Quintile	59.3	7.6	26.6	6.5	100
2nd Quintile	54.1	2.3	38.1	5.5	100
3rd Quintile	43.9	7.4	41.7	7.0	100
4th Quintile	44.5	1.8	41.3	12.4	100
Top Quintile	35.7	3.4	42.5	18.3	100
All Households	47.6	4.5	38.0	9.9	100
					(N=616)

[1] Rounding errors mean that rows will not always sum to exactly 100.0%
Key: Income quintiles group households on the basis of their total disposable incomes:

Bottom quintile:	Lowest	-	£127.94 per week
2nd quintile:	£127.95	-	£185.94 per week
3rd quintile:	£185.95	-	£247.27 per week
4th quintile:	£247.28	-	£329.42 per week
Top quintile:	£329.43	-	highest per week

Appendix D

Table D9 Financial Management Systems: Differences by Social Class

Social Class	Whole Wage System	Allowance System	Joint Management	Independent Management	Total[1]
		Per Cent			
1: Higher Prof.	18.3	7.3	54.6	19.8	100
2: Lower Prof.	47.7	1.0	34.3	17.1	100
3: Non-Manual	58.5	1.0	30.3	10.2	100
4: Skilled Manual	47.8	5.7	36.9	9.6	100
5: Semi-Skilled Manual	57.2	6.9	35.2	0.6	100
6: Unskilled Manual	56.3	2.3	38.0	3.4	100
All Households	**47.6**	**4.5**	**38.0**	**9.9**	**100** (N=616)

[1] Rows will not always sum to exactly 100.0% due to rounding errors.

Key:

Social Class 1   Higher professional employees and self-employed; senior managers; larger proprietors; farmers with 200 or more acres.

Social Class 2   Lower professional employees; junior managers; small proprietors; farmers with 100-199 acres.

Social Class 3   Intermediate and other non-manual employees; farmers with 50-99 acres.

Social Class 4   Skilled manual employees and farmers with 30-49 acres.

Social Class 5   Semi-Skilled manual employees and farmers with less than 30 acres.

Social Class 6   Unskilled manual employees.

Table D10 Financial Management Systems: Differences by Special Household
Characteristics.

Household Characteristics	Whole Wage System	Allowance System	Joint Management	Independent Management	Total[1]
			Per Cent		
Farming Main Income Source	59.2	0.5	33.4	7.0	100 (N=73)
Welfare Payments GT 50% of Income	62.7	6.6	27.1	3.6	100 (N=149)
Wife in Employment	41.7	4.4	27.7	26.3	100 (N=147)
All Households	**47.6**	**4.5**	**38.0**	**9.9**	**100** (N=616)

[1] Rows may not sum to exactly 100.0% due to rounding errors.

Appendix D

Table D11 Financial Management Systems: Differences by Family Cycle Stage

Family Cycle Stage	Whole Wage System	Allowance System	Joint Management	Independent Management	Total[1]
			Per Cent		
1: No Children, Young Parents.	59.3	0.0	26.1	14.6	100
2: Child < 5	44.5	4.4	39.8	11.3	100
3: Child 5 - 15	48.7	5.3	41.3	4.7	100
4: Child > 15	45.7	5.7	37.7	10.9	100
5: No Children Middle age parents	57.2	4.6	25.8	12.5	100
6: No Children Retired parents	48.1	3.0	36.1	12.8	100
All Households	**47.6**	**4.5**	**38.0**	**9.9**	**100** (N=616)

[1] Rows will not always sum to exactly 100.0% due to rounding errors.
Key:
Family Cycle Stage 1: Young married; no children in household.
Family Cycle Stage 2: Child less than 5 years old present.
Family Cycle Stage 3: Child between 5 and 15 years old present.
Family Cycle Stage 4: Child older than 15 present.
Family Cycle Stage 5: No children present; husband 40 to 65 years old and wife older than 45.
Family Cycle Stage 6: No children present; husband aged 66 plus and wife older than 45.

Table D12 Income Sharing in Irish Households: Averages by Income Quintile, Social
Class, Family Cycle, and Special Household Characteristics.

Characteristics	Average Percentage Of Income Shared	Standard Deviation	N
Income Quintile[1]	**Per Cent**		
Bottom	40	(.38)	119
2nd	56	(.36)	120
3rd	70	(.28)	119
4th	59	(.27)	119
Top	50	(.28)	110
Social Class[1]			
1: High Professional	56	(.33)	77
2: Lower Professional	60	(.32)	68
3: Non-manual	63	(.31)	90
4: Skilled Manual	56	(.34)	195
5: Semi-skilled Manual	48	(.33)	97
6: Unskilled Manual	50	(.35)	57
Family Cycle Stage[1]			
1: No children			
Young Parents	68	(.24)	28
2: Child < 5	58	(.37)	204
3: Child 5 - 15	61	(.32)	154
4: Child > 15	49	(.22)	109
5: No children			
Middle age parents	54	(.34)	30
6: No children			
Retired parents	36	(.35)	62
Special Household Characteristics[1]			
Farm Household	61	(.24)	70
Social Welfare GT 50%	33	(.34)	146
Wife in Employment	59	(.29)	140
All Households	**55**		

[1] For full keys see Tables D5, D9, D10 and D11.

Appendix D

Table D13 Groceries as a Percentage of Shared Income: Averages by Income Quintile, Social Class, Family Cycle and Special Household Characteristics.

Characteristics	Groceries as a Percentage of Shared Income	Standard Deviation	N
Income Quintile[1]	Per Cent		
Bottom	85	(.46)	69
2nd	62	(.30)	92
3rd	55	(.27)	112
4th	56	(.29)	115
Top	48	(.24)	105
Social Class[1]			
1: High Professional	52	(.27)	68
2: Lower Professional	49	(.23)	63
3: Non-manual	56	(.31)	64
4: Skilled Manual	62	(.34)	160
5: Semi-skilled Manual	66	(.40)	74
6: Unskilled Manual	68	(.30)	42
Family Cycle Stage[1]			
1: No children			
Young Parents	48	(.27)	28
2: Child < 5	52	(.27)	163
3: Child 5 - 15	58	(.36)	135
4: Child > 15	68	(.28)	107
5: No children			
Middle age parents	68	(.54)	24
6: No children			
Retired parents	70	(.29)	36
Special Household Characteristics[1]			
Farm Household	79	(.58)	64
Social Welfare GT 50%	86	(.49)	102
Wife in Employment	51	(.22)	122
All Households	**59**	**(.32)**	**491**

[1] For full keys see Tables D5, D9, D10 and D11.

Table D14 Disagreement Between Spouses on Financial Matters

Number of Disagreements	Financial Management System				Total
	Whole Wage System	Allowance System	Joint Management	Independent Management	
	Per Cent				
None	65.2	69.0	67.0	63.7	65.9
One	28.9	23.6	26.3	30.6	27.9
Two	3.9	7.3	2.4	4.0	4.1
Three	1.4	0.0	2.8	1.7	2.0
Four	0.7	0.0	1.4	0.0	0.9
Total	100.0 (N=285)	100.0 (N=28)	100.0 (N=231)	100.0 (N=60)	100.0 (N=604)

Table D15 Who Would Decide on How to Resolve a Financial Emergency: Husband and Wife Responses by Financial Management System

Who Decides	Financial Management System				Total
	Whole Wage System	Allowance System	Joint Management	Independent Management	
	Per Cent				
Husband	7.8	24.0	10.1	18.4	10.2
Wife	5.8	8.7	4.2	3.8	5.2
Joint	70.6	27.3	59.8	60.2	64.9
Disagree	15.8	40.0	25.9	17.6	19.6
Total	100.0 (N=290)	100.0 (N=17)	100.0 (N=142)	100.0 (N=61)	100.0 (N=510)

Appendix D

Table D16 Access to Personal Spending Money: Husband and Wife Responses by Financial Management System

	Financial Management System				Total
	Whole Wage System	Allowance System	Joint Management	Independent Management	
	Per Cent				
Husband Yes/Wife No	20.0	23.7	19.4	5.9	18.5
Husband No/Wife Yes	6.6	0.0	3.2	4.6	4.8
Both Yes	50.9	66.3	60.2	73.2	57.4
Both No	22.5	10.0	17.5	16.3	19.4
Total	**100.0** (N=288)	**100.0** (N=27)	**100.0** (N=230)	**100.0** (N=61)	**100.0** (N= 606)

Table D17 Wives' Personal Expenditure Money by Financial Management System

Financial Management System	Wife's Average Personal Expenditure Money	Standard Deviation	N
Whole Wage System (One Person Management)	£ 10.67	7.7	161
Allowance System (Main Earner Control)	£ 6.20	2.9	18
Joint Management	£ 12.35	12.8	147
Independent Management	£ 22.06	20.1	47
All Households			**373**

Table D18 Did You Have an Afternoon or Evening Out in Last Fortnight?: Differences by Financial Management System

	Financial Management System				Total
	Whole Wage System	**Allowance System**	**Joint Management**	**Independent Management**	
	Per Cent				
Husband Yes/Wife No	14.3	32.3	16.0	15.3	15.8
Husband No/Wife Yes	11.1	4.7	10.0	2.8	9.6
Both Yes	39.0	49.2	49.2	71.8	46.6
Both No	35.6	13.8	24.7	10.2	28.0
Total	**100.0**	**100.0**	**100.0**	**100.0**	**100.0**
	(N=291)	(N=27)	(N=233)	(N=61)	(N= 612)

Appendix D

Table D19 Households with Dependent Children: Wives' Income Status by Social Class and Total Household Income[1]

	No Independent Income	Earnings LT Child Benefit	Earnings GT Child Benefit	Total	N
Social Class		**Per Cent**			
1: Higher Professional	42.2	13.5	44.3	100	(63)
2: Lower Professional	59.7	9.5	30.8	100	(49)
3: Non-manual	53.8	13.0	33.2	100	(56)
4: Skilled Manual	57.1	12.5	30.3	100	(143)
5: Semi-skilled Manual	64.4	0.7	34.9	100	(62)
6: Unskilled Manual	80.4	3.8	15.8	100	(40)
Income Quintile					
Bottom	81.8	5.2	13.0	100	83
2nd	75.8	7.0	17.3	100	83
3rd	63.9	12.2	23.7	100	84
4th	37.1	10.7	52.2	100	82
Top	32.0	13.3	54.7	100	82 (N=414)

[1] For full key see Tables D5 and D9.

Table D20 How Women's Income is Usually Spent?

Purpose	Per Cent
Clothes, shoes for yourself	9.0
Recreation for yourself	4.9
Clothes, shoes for children	5.1
School Expenses	1.6
Regular bills (gas, ESB, rent, etc)	8.7
General Housekeeping	62.3
Other	8.0
Total	**100.0**

Table D21 Distribution of Women's Income by Purpose: Families With and Without Dependent Children

	0%	1-10%	11-25%	26-50%	51-75%	76%+	Total
With Children							
Personal Consumption	30.7	34.9	16.9	17.3	0.4	0.0	100%
Children	45.9	24.2	14.3	12.3	3.3	0.0	100%
General Household	5.8	2.1	0.2	20.9	18.1	52.7	100%
							(N=108)
Without Children							
Personal Consumption	12.0	30.8	47.4	7.5	2.2	0.0	100%
Children	92.2	1.4	4.6	1.7	0.0	0.0	100%
General Household	0.0	0.8	2.3	25.6	19.2	52.2	100%
							(N=68)

Notes:
1. Each row in the table refers to one of the three spending areas and indicates the distribution of women according to the proportion of their incomes allocated to specific spending areas.
2. Rows may not sum to exactly 100% due to rounding errors.

Table D22 Who Decides How to Spend the Child Benefit?

	Per Cent	(N)
Usually Wife	77.3	(280)
Usually Husband	0.6	(2)
Usually Joint Decision	22.1	(80)
Total	**100.0**	**(367)**

Appendix D

Table D23 Use of Child Benefit by Decision Maker

Use of Child Benefit	Decision Maker		Households Receiving Child Benefit[1]
	Wife	**Jointly**	
	Per Cent		
General Housekeeping	26.2	30.7	27.0
Regular Bills	19.5	43.8	24.8
Shoes, Cloths for Children	40.9	16.9	35.3
School Expenses	3.4	1.2	2.9
Other	10.0	7.4	10.0
Total	**100.0**	**100.0**	**100.0**
	(N=279)	(N=80)	(N=359)

[1] All households receiving Child Benefit and responding to this question.

Table D24 Control and Use of Child Benefit: Differences by Financial Management
System[1]

| | Financial Management System | | | |
	Whole Wage System	Allowance System	Joint Management	Independent Management
	Per Cent			
Control of Child Benefit:				
Decided by				
Usually Wife	73.5	59.5	85.6	70.8
Usually Joint	25.5	40.5	14.4	29.2
	100.0	100.0	100.0	100.0
	(N=165)	(N=18)	(N=144)	(N=32)
Use of Child Benefit:				
General Housekeeping	31.9	24.0	25.7	11.8
Regular Bills	28.2	58.0	18.0	14.9
Children's Clothing	25.5	14.3	44.2	54.2
School	2.4	0.0	2.7	8.5
Other	12.0	3.6	9.3	10.6
Total	**100.0**	**100.0**	**100.0**	**100.0**
	(N=163)	(N=18)	(N=144)	(N=52)

[1] The table includes only those households currently receiving Child Benefit payments. Two households reporting that the husband usually decides on how Child Benefit is spent are omitted from the table. Both households fall under the "Allowance System" of financial management.

Appendix D

Table D25 Wives' Priorities for Spending an Additional £20 per week[1]

Spending Priorities	Whole Wage System	Allowance System	Joint Management	Independent Management
	Per Cent			
Food	26.2	25.3	22.0	3.6
Children's Clothing	23.5	27.5	23.4	27.0
Adult Clothing	4.0	4.6	6.8	2.7
Regular Bills	20.2	6.5	11.2	21.5
School Expenses	1.4	0.0	4.2	0.0
Debts	11.7	13.9	12.6	30.5
Savings	5.2	0.0	8.4	13.9
House Improvements	3.9	10.7	5.9	0.8
Holiday	1.7	11.6	4.1	0.0
Other	2.0	0.0	1.4	0.0
Total	**100.0**	**100.0**	**100.0**	**100.0**
	(N=199)	(N=20)	(N=179)	(N=37)

[1] Married couples with resident children by financial management system.

Table D26 Husbands' Priorities for Spending an Additional £20 per week[1]

Spending Priorities	Whole Wage System	Allowance System	Joint Management	Independent Management
	Per Cent			
Food	18.6	30.4	18.9	11.8
Children's Clothing	13.1	34.2	13.0	5.7
Adult Clothing	4.8	2.3	1.3	1.4
Regular Bills	24.2	5.2	14.6	30.5
School Expenses	4.6	11.6	7.2	0.0
Debts	10.9	12.2	17.0	28.5
Savings	10.9	2.4	14.2	16.0
House Improvements	6.1	1.7	7.7	5.3
Holiday	2.7	0.0	2.1	0.0
Other	3.9	0.0	3.9	0.9
Total	**100.0**	**100.0**	**100.0**	**100.0**
	(N=196)	(N=20)	(N=178)	(N=38)

[1] Married couples with resident children by financial management system.

Bibliography

ALLAN, G (1989) *Friendship: Developing a Sociological Perspective*, London: Harvester Wheatsheaf.

BRANNEN, J & P MOSS (1987) "Dual earner households: women's financial contributions after the birth of the first child". Pp 75 - 95 in J BRANNEN and G WILSON (eds) *Give and Take in Families: Studies in Resource Distribution*. London: Allen & Unwin.

BREEN, R, D HANNAN, D ROTTMAN and C WHELAN (1990) *Understanding Contemporary Ireland: State, Class, and Development in the Republic of Ireland*. London: Macmillan.

BREEN, R, C T WHELAN and B J WHELAN (1992) "Industrialisation, Class Formation and Social Mobility in Ireland". Pp 105-128 in J GOLDTHORPE and C T WHELAN (eds) *The Development of Industrial Society in Ireland*, Proceedings of the British Academy. Oxford University Press: Oxford.

BRYANT, W K (1990) *The Economic Organization of the Household*. Cambridge: Cambridge University Press.

BURGOYNE, C B (1990) "Money in marriage: how patterns of allocation both reflect and conceal power". *Sociological Review* 38 No 4: 634-65

CALLAN, T, B NOLAN, D HANNAN, B J WHELAN and S CREIGHTON (1988) *Poverty and the Social Welfare System in Ireland*, Dublin: Combat Poverty Agency.

CALLAN, T, B NOLAN and B WHELAN, D HANNAN with S CREIGHTON (1989) *Poverty, Income and Welfare in Ireland*. Dublin: Economic and Social Research Institute, General Research Series No 146

CENTRAL STATISTICS OFFICE (1987) Census 1986, *Summary Population Report, 1987*. Dublin: Stationery Office

CENTRAL STATISTICS OFFICE (1989) *Household Budget Survey 1987*. Dublin: Stationery Office

CENTRAL STATISTICS OFFICE (1989) Census 1986, *Summary Population Report - 2nd Series*. Dublin: Stationery Office.

CENTRAL STATISTICS OFFICE (1993) *Statistical Bulletin* Vol LXV111 No 2. Dublin: Stationery Office.

COSER, R L (1990) "Power lost and status gained: a step in the direction of sex equality". Pp 71-87 in K ERIKSON and S VALLAS (eds) *The Nature of Work: Sociological Perspectives*. New Haven: Yale University Press.

145

DALY, M (1989) *Women and Poverty*. Dublin: Attic Press, in conjunction with the Combat Poverty Agency.

ERIKSON, R and J H GOLDTHORPE (1992) *The Constant Flux: A Study of Class Mobility in Industrial Societies*. Oxford: Clarendon Press.

FITZGERALD, E (1992) *Commentary on Review Body on the Treatment of Households in the Social Welfare Code*. Dublin: Report to the Combat Poverty Agency.

GOLDTHORPE, J (1987) *Social Mobility and Class Structure in Modern Britain: Second Edition*. Oxford: Clarendon Press.

GOVERNMENT OF IRELAND (1984) *Building on Reality 1985-1987*. Dublin: Stationery Office.

GRAHAM, H (1987) "Women's poverty and caring". Pp 221-240 in C GLENDINNING and J MILLAR (eds) *Women and Poverty in Britain*. Brighton: Wheatsheaf.

HANNAN, D and L KATSIAOUNI (1977) *Traditional Families? From Culturally Prescribed to Negotiated Roles in Farm Families*. Dublin: Economic and Social Research Institute.

HILL, W and J SCANZONI (1982) "An approach for assessing marital decision-making processes". *Journal of Marriage and the Family 44* No 4:927-941

HUMPHREYS, A J (1966) *New Dubliners: Urbanization and the Irish Family*. London: Routledge and Kegan Paul.

JENKINS, S P (1991) "Poverty measurement and the within-household distribution: agenda for action". *Journal of Social Policy 20*, Part 4: 457-483.

JOWELL, R, S WITHERSPOON, and L BROOK (1987) *British Social Attitudes: the 1984 Report*. London: Social and Community Planning Research.

KENNEDY, F (1989) *Family, Economy and Government in Ireland*. Dublin: Economic and Social Research Institute, General Research Series No 143.

LAND, H (1983) "Poverty and gender: the distribution of family resources". Pp 49-71 in M BROWN (ed) *The Structure of Disadvantage*. London: Heinemann.

LAURIE, H (1991) "Methodological issues in the study of household allocative systems". *Working Papers of the ESRC Research Centre on Micro-social Change Paper 5*. Colchester: University of Essex.

LAZEAR, E P and R T MICHAEL (1988) *Allocation of Income Within the Household*. Chicago: University of Chicago Press.

LE PLAY, F (1879) "Les Ouvriers Europeens". Paris. S Dupertius (tr). In C ZIMMERMAN and M FRAMPTON (eds). *Family and Society.* New York: Van Nostrand, 1935.

LEE J J (1989) *Ireland 1912-1985: Politics and Society.* Cambridge: Cambridge University Press.

LEE, P and M GIBNEY (1989) *Patterns of Food and Nutrient Intake in a Suburb of Dublin with Chronically High Unemployment.* Dublin: Combat Poverty Agency, Research Report Series No 2.

LISTER, R (1990) "Women, economic dependency and citizenship". *Journal of Social Policy 19* No 4:445-467

McKEE, L and C BELL (1986) "His unemployment, her problem: the domestic and marital consequences of male unemployment". Pp 135-149 in S ALLEN, A WATON, K PURCELL and S WOOD (eds) *The Experience of Unemployment.* London: Macmillan.

McRAE, S (1987) "The allocation of money in cross-class families". *The Sociological Review 35* No 1:97-122.

MILLMAN, M (1991) *Warm Hearts and Cold Cash: the Intimate Dynamics of Families and Money.* New York: The Free Press.

MORRIS, L (1990) *The Workings of the Household: A US-UK Comparison.* Cambridge: Polity Press.

MORRIS, L D (1984) "Redundancy and patterns of household finance". *The Sociological Review 32* No 3:492-523.

MORRIS, L and S RUANE (1989) *Household Finance Management and the Labour Market.* Aldershot: Avebury.

MOSER, C A and G KALTON (1971) *Survey Methods in Social Investigation. 2nd Edition.* New York: Basic Books

NATIONAL ECONOMIC and SOCIAL COUNCIL (1990) *A Strategy for the Nineties: Economic Stability and Structural Change.* Dublin: NESC (Pl. 7619).

NOLAN, B. (1991) *The Wealth of Irish Households: What Can We Learn from Survey Data?* Dublin: Combat Poverty Agency.

O'CONNOR, P (1991) "Women's experience of power within marriage: an inexplicable phenomenon". *Sociological Review 39* No 4:823-842

O'HARE, A, C T WHELAN, and P COMMINS (1991) "The Development of an Irish Census-Based Social Class Scale". *Economic and Social Review 22* No 2:135-156

PAHL, J (1983) "The allocation of money and the structuring of inequality within marriage". *Sociological Review 31* No 2:237-262

PAHL, J (1989) *Money and Marriage*. London: Macmillan.

PAHL, J (1990) "Household spending, personal spending and the control of money in marriage". *Sociology 24* No 1:119-138

PAHL, J (1991) "Money and power in marriage". Pp. 41-57 in P ABBOTT and L WALLACE (eds) *Gender, Power and Sexuality*. London: Macmillan.

PIACHAUD, D. (1987) "The distribution of income and work". *Oxford Review of Economic Policy 3*. No 3:41-61

RAINWATER, L, M REIN and J SCHWARTZ (1986) *Income Packaging in the Welfare State: A Comparative Study of Family Income*. Oxford: Clarendon Press.

REVIEW GROUP ON THE TREATMENT OF HOUSEHOLDS IN THE SOCIAL WELFARE CODE (1991) *Report*. Dublin: Stationery Office.

ROGERS, B and N P SCHLOSSMAN (1990) *Intra-Household Resource Allocation: Issues and Methods for Development Policy and Planning*. Tokyo: United Nations University Press.

ROSE, D and H LAURIE (1991) "Household allocative systems, gender and class analysis". *Working Papers of the ESRC Research Centre on Micro-social Change Paper 6.* Colchester: University of Essex.

ROTTMAN, D, D HANNAN, N HARDIMAN and M WILEY (1982) *The Distribution of Income in the Republic of Ireland: A Study in Social Class and Family-Cycle Inequalities*. Dublin: The Economic Social Research Institute, General Research Series No 109.

ROTTMAN, D and M REIDY (1988) *Redistribution Through State Social Expenditure in the Republic of Ireland: 1973-1980*. Dublin: National Economic and Social Council.

ROWNTREE, B S (1899) *Poverty: A Study of Town Life*. London: Macmillan.

SCHANINGER, C and W BUSS (1986) "A longitudinal comparison of consumption and finance handling between happily married and divorced couples". *Journal of Marriage and the Family 48* No 1:129-136.

SMITH, D J (1992) "The future of the underclass". Pp. 88-95 in D SMITH (ed) *Understanding the Underclass*. London: Policy Studies Institute.

SMITH, S (ed) (1991) *Economic Policy and the Division of Income Within the Family*. London: The Institute for Fiscal Studies.

SPITZE, G (1988) "Women's employment and family relations: a review". *Journal of*

Marriage and the Family 50 No 3:595-618.

STAMP, P (1985) "Balance of financial power in marriage: an exploratory study of breadwinning wives". *The Sociological Review 33* No. 3:546-557.

TAYLOR-GOOBY, P (1985) "Personal consumption and gender: an analysis of national survey data and the relationship between standards of living, gender, marital status and work". *Sociology 19* No 2:273-284.

THOMAS, D (1990) "Intra-household resource allocation: an inferential approach". *Journal of Human Resources 25* No 4:635-664.

TOWNSEND, P (1979) *Poverty in the United Kingdom.* Harmondsworth: Penguin.

VOGLER, C (1989) "Labour Market Change and Patterns of Financial Allocation within Households". *ESRC Working Paper 12: The Social Change and Life Initiative.*

WHELAN, B J (1979) "RANSAM: A Random Sample Design for Ireland". *The Economic and Social Review 10* pp 169-174.

WHELAN, C T and B J WHELAN (1984) *Social Mobility in the Republic of Ireland: A Comparative Perspective. Dublin. Economic and Social Research Institute,* General Research Series Paper No 116.

WHELAN, C T and D F HANNAN, S CREIGHTON (1991) *Unemployment, Poverty and Psychological Distress.* Dublin: Economic and Social Research Institute, General Research Series Paper No 150.

WILLIAMS, J and B J WHELAN (1994) *The Dynamics of Poverty: Short Term Issues in Poverty Transitions.* Dublin: Combat Poverty Agency.

WILSON, G (1987) *Money in the Family: Financial Organisation and Women's Responsibility.* Aldershot: Avebury.

YOUNG, M and P WILLMOTT (1957) *Family and Kin in East London.* London: Routledge and Kegan Paul.

YOUNG, M (1952) "Distribution of income within the family". *British Journal of Sociology 3*, pp 305-321.

YOUNG, M (1977) "Housekeeping money" in F WILLIAMS (ed.) *Why the Poor Pay More.* London: Macmillan.

ZELIZER, V A (1989) "The social meaning of monies: 'special monies'". *American Journal of Sociology 95* No 2:342-377.

ZWEIG, F (1961) *The Worker in an Affluent Society.* London: Heinemann Educational Books.

Combat Poverty Agency Publications

Research Report Series

No. 1   T.R. GORMLEY et al (1989); Assessment of School Meals and Growth, Food Intake and Food Likes/Dislikes of Primary School Children in Inner City Dublin Schools; £2.00.

No. 2   P. LEE and M. GIBNEY (1989); Patterns of Food and Nutrient Intake in a Suburb of Dublin with Chronically High Unemployment; £2.00.

No. 3   B. DILLON (1989); A Review and Recent History of the Coolock Community Law Centre; £2.00.

No. 4   B. CULLEN(1989); Poverty, Community and Development; £3.00.

No. 5   S. BYRNE (1990); Wealth and the Wealthy in Ireland; £2.00.

No. 6   P. WARD (1990); Financial Consequences of Marital Breakdown; £4.00.

No. 7   B. NOLAN and B. FARRELL (1990); Child Poverty in Ireland; £4.00.

No. 8   L. HAYES (1990); Working for Change, A Study of Three Women's Community Projects; £4.00.

No. 9   D. DONNISON et al (1991); Urban Poverty, the Economy and Public Policy; £5.00.

No. 10 F. MILLS et al (1991); Scheme of Last Resort?: a review of Supplementary Welfare Allowance; £6.00.

No. 11 C. MULVEY (1991); Report on the Department of Social Welfare's Grants Scheme for Locally based Women's Groups; £2.00.

No.12   B. NOLAN (1991); The Wealth of Irish Households; £6.00.

No. 13 P. KELLEHER and M. WHELAN (1992); Dublin Communities in Action; A Study of Six Projects; (with Community Action Network); £6.00.

No. 14 J. MURPHY LAWLESS (1992); The Adequacy of Income and Family Expenditure; £6.00.

No. 15 J. MILLAR, S. LEEPER, C. DAVIES (1992); Lone Parents, Poverty and Public Policy in Ireland; £6.00.

No. 16 J. WILLIAMS and B. WHELAN, (1994); The Dynamics of Poverty; £6.00.

No. 17 C. CARNEY et al (1994); The Cost of a Child; £6.00.

No. 18 D. ROTTMAN(1994); Income Distribution Within Households; £6.00.

Recent Policy Documents

Towards a Policy for Combating Poverty among Women (1990); £3.00.

Poverty - An Agenda for the '90s (1989), Free.

Tackling Poverty in the Nineties (1990), Free.

Making Social Rights a Reality (1991), Free.

Building a Fairer Future (1992), Free

Education, Inequality and Poverty (1993), Free

A Programme for Social Equity (1993), Free

A Budget for Social Inclusion (1993), Free

Poverty & Policy 1, B. Nolan (1993); Reforming Child Income Support; £1.00.

A complete list of Agency publications, including resource materials, conference reports and policy statements, is available from the Agency at 8 Charlemont Street, Dublin 2.